The Chocolate Lovers' Cookbook

TORMONT

The Chocolate Lovers' Cookbook

Compiled by Juliet Cobb

Photography by Ashley Barber
Home economist: Kay Francis

Handmade chocolate recipes by Jilly Brain and Dale Wohler
Handmade chocolates tested by Ruth Hewitt

This edition is published with the permission of
HarperCollins Publishers Pty Limited.

Published in 1994 by
Tormont Publications Inc.
338 Saint Antoine St. East
Montreal, Canada H2Y 1A3
Tel. (514) 954-1441
Fax (514) 954-1443
ISBN 2-89429-390-9
Printed in Canada

CONTENTS

INTRODUCTION

Chocolate is one of life's great pleasures. Its rich consistency and distinctive flavor appeal to almost everyone's sweet tooth. It is also a prime source of instant energy as it is full of carbohydrates and contains traces of the stimulants caffeine and theobromine.

This book teaches you how to make your own handmade chocolates with individual illustrations, step-by-step recipes and easy-to-follow methods. There are simple recipes for beginners, or you can make more sophisticated chocolates to round off a special occasion with real style. And there are chocolate cookies, cakes, layer cakes, and every kind of exotic dessert.

Chocolate was first brought to the western world 400 years ago, when Spanish explorers came across it in South America. At first it was used only as a drink, but in the 19th century the familiar chocolate bar was invented in Switzerland and quickly became the world's most popular confection.

The tree that yields chocolate is aptly named *Theobroma*, which means 'food of the gods.' The tree has been cultivated for so many centuries that there are probably no wild trees left. It is from the pale purple-pink beans within the pulp of the hanging fruit that chocolate is made. The beans are fermented, dried, roasted and processed into a paste called chocolate liquor. Chocolate liquor is richly colored and bitter, and is not generally available as it is difficult to cook with.

Cocoa powder is made by pressing the cocoa butter (vegetable fat) out of the pure chocolate liquor and then pulverizing the remains. Extra cocoa butter has to be added to chocolate liquor to turn it into block chocolate or compound chocolate. Cocoa has less fat and sugar than block chocolate, but also less of the true chocolate flavor.

The less sweet, good quality dark or plain chocolate blocks are satisfactory for cooking, or you can use a good quality baking chocolate. Chocolate with a fairly high cocoa butter content has more fluidity and won't ball around the spoon when melting. Thick, chunky chocolate may not melt quite as easily as thinner blocks, but some cooking chocolate is labelled easy-to-melt. If chocolate is not melting easily, add a little copha fat (2 to 3 percent of weight of chocolate) shortening, or vegetable oil.

For handmade chocolates, look for compound chocolate or couverture chocolate.

Chocolate Almond Cream Flan
(recipe page 40)

How to Make the Most of Chocolate

Chocolate Drinks

For chocolate-flavored liquid (i.e. hot or cold chocolate drinks), allow 4 oz (110 g) chocolate for every 4 cups (1 L) of liquid. Chop chocolate into liquid and allow it to melt slowly over low heat. The result will be a deliciously thick, velvety mixture.

You can substitute ¾ cup (185 mL) cocoa powder and ¼ cup (60 mL) sugar per 4 oz (110 g) chocolate, if you prefer.

If you wish to drink the chocolate mixture cold, bear in mind that it will thicken considerably as it cools.

Chocolate Custard

Melt chocolate in the milk as it heats and proceed as usual.

Grating Chocolate

Before grating chocolate, place it and a measuring cup in the fridge for an hour or so. Grate chocolate into the cold measuring cup so it can be measured easily, without melting, as you go along. Do not touch grated chocolate, as it will melt immediately with the warmth of your hand.

Chopping Chocolate

The easiest way to chop chocolate is to break the slab into smallish pieces on a large board. Press down on back of knife blade as you chop.

Chocolate and Cream

To melt chocolate in fresh heavy cream, put cream in a heavy-based saucepan and heat over very low heat. Add pieces of chocolate and stir until just melted. Allow to cool and then beat by hand or with an electric beater. The cream will double in volume and become rich and light in texture. Use immediately to cover cakes or desserts before it hardens.

Orange and Chocolate Soufflé
(recipe page 37)

Cooking with Chocolate

• When a recipe calls for melted chocolate, it must be heated in a bowl or on a plate suspended over (but definitely not in) a pan of hot, but not boiling, water. Overheated chocolate has a bitter taste and loses its glossy shine and delicious aroma.

• Melt chocolate slowly without stirring, although some cooks advocate working it with a thin metal spatula if it is to be used for coating cakes or making chocolate cases, because that helps it keep its gloss when it sets. The chocolate should be no more than lukewarm.

• Chop or break chocolate into small pieces before melting so it melts quickly and evenly. Do not stir chocolate while it melts.

• Test that chocolate is melted by dipping the point of a knife into the center.

• Cool chocolate at room temperature, because this also helps to maintain the gloss.

• Be careful that not even a drop of water gets into the bowl (unless this is part of the recipe). Water prevents a good sheen and will make the chocolate thick.

• Remember that instant chocolate milk powder (drinking chocolate) and cocoa are not interchangeable; drinking chocolate has a milder, sweeter flavor.

Storing Handmade Chocolates

• Do not refrigerate handmade chocolates or they will discolor and will sweat when you remove them from the fridge.

• The handmade chocolates in this book will keep for 2 to 3 weeks – although those made with cream have a shorter shelf life. However, it is unlikely that anything as tempting as handmade chocolates will last that long!

Handmade Chocolates
(see page 69)

SAUCES

Quick Rich Chocolate Sauce

2 tbsp (30 mL) cocoa
*   powder*
1 cup (250 mL) brown
*   sugar*
1 tbsp (15 mL) butter
pinch salt
1 cup (250 mL) cream

Boil all ingredients together for a few minutes. Serve immediately over pancakes or crêpes, ice cream, or fresh or stewed fruit.

Makes 2 cups (500 mL)

Basic Chocolate Sauce

This simple, rich, smooth chocolate sauce can be served with freshly baked brioches or with puddings, fruit or ice cream.

6 oz (170 g) dark or
*   semisweet baking chocolate*
½ cup (125 mL) sugar
2½ cups (625 mL) water

Cut chocolate into small pieces and melt in a bowl over a pan of hot water.

Heat sugar and water in saucepan, stirring constantly until sugar dissolves. Boil syrup gently for 5 minutes.

Carefully stir sugar syrup into chocolate. Return mixture to saucepan and, stirring continuously, bring it to a simmer. Let it simmer for 7-10 minutes or until sauce thickly coats back of a wooden spoon.

Makes 2½ cups (625 mL)

Creamy Chocolate Sauce

½ cup (125 mL) chocolate
*   milk powder*
1 cup (250 mL)
*   evaporated milk*
1 tbsp (15 mL) golden
*   syrup or corn syrup*
½ tsp (2 mL) vanilla
*   extract*
2 tsp (10 mL) butter

In a saucepan, combine chocolate milk powder with evaporated milk and syrup. Bring mixture to a boil over medium heat, stirring constantly. Simmer 5 minutes. Remove from heat, add vanilla and butter, and serve hot.

Makes 1¼ cups (310 mL)

Chocolate Mint Sauce

A foolproof recipe for chocolate sauce – and really tasty.

12 chocolate-covered
*   peppermint wafers*
½ cup (125 mL) cream

Put peppermint wafers in small bowl over saucepan of boiling water. Allow chocolates to melt. Stir and slowly add cream. Serve warm or cold over ice cream or fruit.

Serves 4

Quick Rich Chocolate Sauce and Crêpes
Tia Maria (recipe page 28)

DESSERTS

Chocolate Banana Sundaes

3 ripe bananas
3 tbsp (45 mL) rum
2½ cups (625 mL) whipping
*   cream*
6 oz (170 g) dark or semisweet
*   baking chocolate, finely grated*
4 scoops vanilla or coffee
*   ice cream*
grated chocolate to garnish

Slice bananas very thinly and sprinkle with rum.

Whip cream until thick. Remove ¼ of the whipped cream and mix it with ½ the chocolate; reserve for decoration. Add bananas and rum to remaining cream, and spoon mixture into 4 individual serving dishes.

Just before serving, top each dish with a scoop of ice cream. Pipe chocolate cream mixture around ice cream and sprinkle grated chocolate on top.

Serves 4

Banana Cream

4 oz (110 g) dark or semisweet baking chocolate
1¼ cups (310 mL) whipping cream
2 large ripe bananas

Reserve 2 squares of chocolate and melt remainder in bowl over pan of hot water. Remove from heat and allow melted chocolate to cool slightly.

Whip cream until it forms stiff peaks, being careful not to overwhip.

Mash bananas and fold them with melted chocolate into cream. Divide banana cream between 4 glasses and grate reserved chocolate thickly over top of each. Chill and serve.

Serves 4

Chocolate Charlotte

1 plain sponge cake
3 tbsp (45 mL) rum
2 eggs, separated
¼ cup (60 mL) sugar
1¼ cups (310 mL) milk
1 oz (30 g) grated dark or semisweet
*   baking chocolate*
2 tbsp (30 mL) gelatine
⅔ cup (165 mL) whipping
*   cream, whipped*

Cut a ½ inch (1 cm) layer off the flat base of the sponge cake. Place top half upside-down in a round dish or bowl. Sprinkle with rum.

Cream egg yolks with sugar until pale and fluffy.

Bring milk to a boil in a thick-bottomed pan. Stir in chocolate until melted. Pour milk into egg mixture, stirring well.

Clean saucepan and return mixture to it, cooking over low heat and stirring all the time until mixture coats back of spoon. Remove from heat and add gelatine, stirring until it is dissolved. Leave to cool, stirring from time to time until almost set.

In a separate bowl, beat cream. Fold it into mixture.

Beat egg whites until stiff, and fold into chocolate mixture.

Pour mixture over rum-flavored sponge cake and top with bottom slice of cake. Chill. Turn out on plate right-side-up and serve with custard or whipped cream.

Note: This recipe can be varied by substituting a liqueur such as Grand Marnier for the rum, or by using a chocolate or coffee-flavored sponge cake. Top of cake can be decorated with whipped cream piped into rosettes.

Serves 4-6

Chocolate Orange Cheesecake (recipe page 32)

Chocolate Cointreau Mousse

This mousse is very rich, and a little goes a long way. It looks attractive served in tiny china bowls or demi-tasse cups, and can then be stretched to serve 6 people.

8 oz (225 g) dark or semisweet baking chocolate
¼ cup (60 mL) strong black coffee
1 tbsp (15 mL) butter
1 tbsp (15 mL) Cointreau

3 large eggs, separated
1 cup (250 mL) whipping cream, whipped, for decoration
caraque curls (see recipe page 72)

Break chocolate into small pieces. Place chocolate and black coffee in top of double boiler or a small bowl standing over a pan of hot water over gentle heat. Stir continuously until chocolate melts and becomes creamy. Cook gently for 2-3 minutes.

Remove bowl from heat and stir in butter and Cointreau until butter dissolves. Cool slightly before beating in egg yolks.

Whisk egg whites until stiff and fold into chocolate mixture. Spoon into glasses or individual dishes and chill in refrigerator until set (about 1 hour). Serve decorated with a swirl of whipped cream and caraque curls.

Serves 4

Melt chocolate and coffee in double boiler

Spoon into individual bowls

Chocolate Castles with Fudgy Sauce

oil for greasing
5 tbsp (75 mL) margarine
⅓ cup (85 mL) sugar
1 egg
½ tsp (2 mL) vanilla
    extract
1 cup (250 mL) self-rising
    flour
¼ cup (60 mL) cocoa
    powder
a little milk to mix

Fudgy Sauce

4 oz (110 g) chocolate
    caramel bars
¼ cup (60 mL) water

Preheat oven to 350°F (180°C). Lightly grease 4 individual custard cups and line base with waxed paper.

Beat margarine and sugar together until pale and fluffy, then beat in egg and vanilla extract. Sift together flour and cocoa powder and fold into creamed mixture with a little milk, to give a soft dropping consistency.

Transfer mixture to prepared custard cups and bake in preheated oven for about 25 minutes, until well risen and firm to the touch.

Just before puddings are cooked, make fudgy sauce; cut up chocolate caramel bars and place in a pan with the water. Stir over gentle heat until bars melt.

Turn out cooked puddings onto individual serving dishes and pour sauce over. Serve hot.

Serves 4

Coffee Cups

1   Sprinkle semolina, coffee
     and sugar into warmed milk

Coffee Cups

2½ cups (625 mL) milk   1 tbsp (15 mL) instant coffee
⅓ cup (85 mL) semolina   ½ cup (125 mL) sugar

Sauce

¼ cup (60 mL) brown   ⅔ cup (165 mL) milk
    sugar   5 tbsp (75 mL) cocoa powder

Warm milk in a pan, then sprinkle in semolina, coffee and sugar. Bring to a boil, stirring continuously and, still stirring, cook for a few more minutes until mixture thickens.

Divide mixture between four ⅔-cup (165 mL) molds than have been rinsed in cold water. Leave to cool and set.

Place all sauce ingredients in a pan. Stir over low heat to dissolve sugar and then boil for a few minutes, stirring continuously until sauce becomes smooth and thick. Serve hot or cold, over turned-out molds.

Note: If you don't have suitable molds, tea cups will do instead. A delicious way of jazzing up this pudding is to stir 1½ tbsp (20 mL) of Tia Maria, Crème de Cacao or brandy into the sauce before pouring it over the molds.

Serves 4

2   When cooked, divide mixture between molds

3   Pour sauce over turned-out molds

Ice Mountain

8 oz (225 g) dark or semisweet
   baking chocolate
3 tbsp (45 mL) sugar
3-4 tbsp (45-60 mL)
   lime juice cordial
½ lb (225 g) plain
   sponge cake
2 eggs, separated
1 cup (250 mL) whipping
   cream

Reserve 2 squares of chocolate and melt the rest with sugar and lime cordial in a bowl over pan of hot water.

Meanwhile, slice sponge cake thinly and use some slices to line a 6-cup (1.5 L) bowl or pudding basin. Fill in gaps with pieces of cake cut to fit.

When chocolate has melted, let it cool slightly and then beat in egg yolks. Whisk egg whites until stiff. In a separate bowl, whisk half the cream until it forms firm peaks. Blend chocolate with whipped cream, then fold in beaten egg whites.

Spoon some chocolate mixture into the bowl so that cake on the bottom is well covered. Arrange a layer of cake on top, again filling gaps, and coat it with a little of the chocolate. Repeat process, ending with sponge cake, until all chocolate has been used up.

Place a plate, the same size as top of bowl, on top. Press it down with weights and leave pudding in refrigerator for a day.

Whip remaining cream. Ease a knife down sides of bowl and turn pudding out on a serving plate. Spread whipped cream over pudding. Grate reserved chocolate and sprinkle it over the top.

Serves 6

Ice Mountain

Chocolate Ice Cream

5 egg yolks
⅔ cup (165 mL) white sugar
2 cups (500 mL) milk
7-8 tbsp (100-120 mL)
  cocoa powder

Whisk egg yolks and sugar until mixture is thick and creamy.

Heat milk in a saucepan, and when it is almost boiling, whisk in cocoa powder. Add boiling chocolate milk gradually to eggs and sugar, stirring continuously, and mix well. Pass mixture through a sieve.

Pour into a clean saucepan, and stir over low heat with a wooden spoon until mixture coats back of spoon. Transfer mixture to an ice cream churn and churn until frozen, or pour into freezer tray and freeze, stirring from time to time.

Press frozen ice cream into a mold and return to freezer. To serve, dip mold in hot water for a few seconds and invert ice cream onto chilled plate.

Serves 6

Gelato Pronto

This is an Italian favorite with layers of ice cream, chocolate sauce and cream.

1 oz (30 g) dark or semisweet
  baking chocolate
1 oz (30 g) milk chocolate
  or coffee-flavored
  chocolate
3 tbsp (45 mL) custard
  powder
½ cup (125 mL) white sugar
7-8 tbsp (100-120 mL)
  cocoa powder
2½ cups (625 mL) milk
1 tsp (5 mL) vanilla extract
1½ cups (375 mL) whipping cream
¾ cup (185 mL) whole
  blanched almonds

Topping

⅔ cup (165 mL) whipping
  cream
1 tbsp (15 mL) sugar
few drops vanilla extract
2 oz (60 g) dark or semisweet
  baking chocolate

Grate dark chocolate into one mixing bowl, and milk or coffee- flavored chocolate into another.

Dissolve custard powder, sugar and cocoa in ¼ of the milk. Heat rest of milk in a pan. Stir in custard mixture and cook for 3 minutes, beating constantly. Add vanilla.

Remove from heat and divide custard between the 2 mixing bowls containing grated chocolate. Stir custard into each one until chocolate is melted.

Allow custard mixtures to cool, beating from time to time to prevent a skin forming. In another bowl, beat whipping cream until thick.

When custards are almost cold, beat half the cream into each one. Place mixtures in 2 freezer trays. Freeze until they start to form ice but are still soft. Transfer to separate bowls and beat thoroughly. Freeze until firm.

To make topping, beat cream with sugar and vanilla. Melt chocolate in a double-boiler over hot water.

When ready to serve, divide scoops of ice cream between 6 ice cream glasses, mixing the 2 flavors. Sprinkle almonds over ice cream balls, reserving 6 for garnishing.

Top each glass with whipped cream, pour melted chocolate over and garnish with a single almond on each. Serve immediately.

Serves 6

Chocolate Orange Trifle

1 chocolate Swiss roll
3 tbsp (45 mL) Grand
  Marnier
2 oranges
2½ cups (625 mL)
  chocolate custard
⅔ cup (165 mL) whipping
  cream, whipped
6 candied cherries,
  halved
2 oz (60 g) grated
  chocolate

Cut Swiss roll into slices about ¾ inch (2 cm) thick and use to line a glass dish as evenly as possible. Sprinkle with Grand Marnier.

Grate rind of one orange and reserve. Peel both oranges and cut in thin slices crosswise, removing pits. Cut slices in half and arrange over cake.

Pour custard over orange and cake slices and chill to set. Beat cream until thick, then fold in grated orange rind. Decorate top of trifle with whipped cream, halved candied cherries and grated chocolate. Serve cold.

Serves 6

Sherry Mocha Dessert

⅔ cup (165 mL) butter
⅔ cup (165 mL) sugar
½ cup (125 mL) cocoa
   powder, sifted
1 cup (250 mL) mixed
   nuts, finely chopped
2 eggs
1 tbsp (15 mL) sherry
1 tbsp (15 mL) cream
¾ cup (185 mL) strong
   black coffee
4 thick slices sponge cake

Decoration

½ lb (225 g) soft butter
3 cups (750 mL) icing
   sugar
1 tbsp (15 mL) cocoa
   powder
¼ cup (60 mL) cream
few drops vanilla extract
1 oz (30 g) chocolate,
   melted
12 roasted hazelnuts

Line with waxed paper the bottom and sides of a large greased loaf pan, and grease paper well.

Cream butter and sugar until light and fluffy. Beat in sifted cocoa, chopped nuts and eggs.

In a clean bowl, mix sherry and cream with strong coffee. Trim 2 sponge cake slices to fit side by side in pan. Brush both slices with coffee mixture and place them in bottom of pan. Spread cocoa butter mixture on top of coffee-soaked cake. Brush remaining cake slices with coffee and press them level on top. Cover and chill overnight.

To make decoration, cream together butter, icing sugar, cocoa, cream, and vanilla extract, adding a little more cream if necessary to give a spreading consistency. Dip base of loaf pan in warm water and turn dessert out on a serving plate. Cut ends to neaten.

Fill a piping bag fitted with a star nozzle with buttercream mixture and pipe over top and sides of cake. Decorate cake with melted chocolate and arrange hazelnuts on top. Serve chilled.

Serves 8

Paradise Ring

20 ladyfingers
1 round sponge cake,
    7 inch (18 cm) diameter
14 oz (400 g) dark or semisweet
    baking chocolate
8 eggs, separated
3 tbsp (45 mL) instant
    coffee
5 tbsp (75 mL) powdered
    gelatine
½ cup (125 mL) hot water
1 cup (250 mL) whipping
    cream
additional chocolate for
    decoration

Lightly grease 8-inch (20 cm) round springform cake pan. Trim ladyfingers to roughly same size. Place sponge cake in center of pan and pack ladyfingers in gap around edge, flat side against cake.

Melt ¾ of the chocolate in a fairly large bowl over pan of hot water. Stir in egg yolks and instant coffee. Dissolve gelatine in hot water and when it is clear, pour into chocolate mixture. Stir and leave to cool slightly.

Whisk egg whites until stiff and fold into chocolate mixture. Turn mixture into prepared pan and leave for several hours to set (see note).

Lightly whip cream until just stiff. Melt remaining chocolate. Spread cream over the chocolate mousse and drizzle on the melted chocolate, swirling it with a skewer to give a marbled effect. Carefully remove sides of pan and slide pudding off base onto a plate. Tie a ribbon around the ladyfingers to keep them in place. Dribble additional melted chocolate over tops of ladyfingers and pipe any remaining cream around base.

Note: Gelatine mixtures tend to toughen in the refrigerator so the ring is better left to set in some other cool place.

Serves 8-10

Place sponge cake in bottom of pan and ladyfingers around sides

Stir egg yolks and instant coffee into melted chocolate

Pour mixture into prepared sponge case

Add vanilla pod to boiled syrup

Turn praline mixture onto metal tray

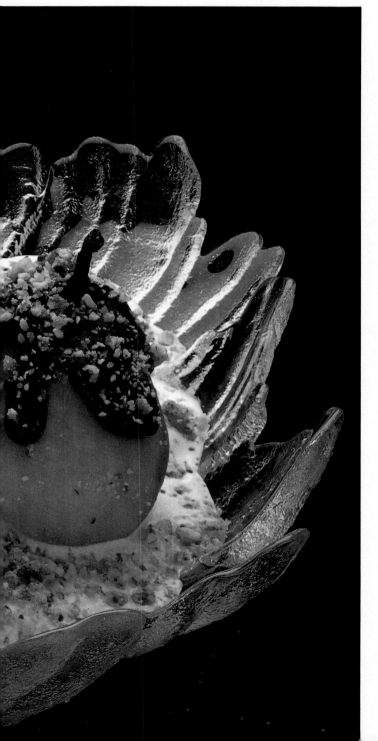

Place pears in baking dish and pour syrup over

Pears Hélène

2½ cups (625 mL) water
1 cup (250 mL) white sugar
1 vanilla pod
4 pears, peeled
1½ cups (375 mL)
    ice cream

Praline

½ cup (125 mL) sugar
1 cup (250 mL) chopped
    nuts
oil for greasing

Chocolate Sauce

8 oz (225 g) dark or semisweet
    baking chocolate
2 cups (500 mL) water
1 tbsp (15 mL) sugar
few drops vanilla extract
¼ cup (60 mL) cream
2 tsp (10 mL) butter

Prepare syrup for pears. Combine water and sugar in a saucepan. Bring gradually to a boil, stirring continuously, until sugar dissolves. Boil syrup for 1 minute and remove from heat. Immediately add vanilla pod. Cover and let syrup slowly cool so it becomes impregnated with vanilla flavor.

While syrup cools, make praline. Place sugar and 1 tbsp (15 mL) water in a heavy-based saucepan. Slowly heat sugar until it begins to caramelize or turn golden. This should happen at 375°F (180°C).

Stir in mixed chopped nuts and turn praline mixture onto a lightly oiled metal tray or shallow cake pan. Allow it to cool. When set, break up and crush into small pieces with a rolling pin.

Preheat oven to 375°F (190°C). Place pears in an ovenproof dish. Remove and discard vanilla pod and pour syrup over pears. Poach pears in oven for 35 minutes, basting and turning frequently to prevent pears browning and drying out. Cover and let them cool in syrup.

To prepare chocolate sauce, dissolve chocolate in water over gentle heat. Stir in sugar and vanilla extract and cook sauce over low heat for 20-25 minutes. Stir in cream and butter and keep sauce hot.

Just before serving, spread ice cream over the bottom of a shallow serving dish. Drain pears and arrange on top. Sprinkle crushed praline over and serve with a bowl of hot chocolate sauce.

Serves 4

Maraschino Charlotte

4 eggs, separated
½ cup (125 mL) granulated
  sugar
2½ cups (625 mL) milk
2 oz (60 g) dark or semisweet
  baking chocolate, chopped
3 tbsp (45 mL) powdered
  gelatine
1¼ cups (310 mL) whipping
  cream
12 ladyfingers
3 tbsp (45 mL) maraschino
  liqueur
6 glacé cherries

Beat egg yolks with sugar until pale and fluffy. Heat milk and stir into yolk mixture. Stir in chopped chocolate until melted. Cook over low heat until mixture coats spoon. Dissolve gelatine in the mixture. Leave it to cool.

Beat ⅔ of cream until stiff and fold into chocolate mixture.

Beat egg whites until stiff and fold into mixture.

Pour a little chocolate mixture into the bottom of a charlotte mold. Sprinkle ladyfingers with maraschino liqueur and arrange around edge of mold.

Pour in remaining chocolate mixture and leave mold in refrigerator until set. Beat remaining cream until stiff. Turn out mold on serving dish and decorate with piped cream and glacé cherries. Serve at once.

Serves 6

Chestnut Mont Blanc

2 x 6 inch (15 cm) square
  sponge cake layers
½ cup (125 mL) rum
3 oz (90 g) dark or semisweet
  baking chocolate
16 oz (450 g) can sweetened
  chestnut purée
⅔ cup (165 mL) whipping
  cream

Sprinkle cake layers with 5 tbsp (75 mL) of the rum.

Melt chocolate in bowl over pan of hot water and stir it into chestnut purée with remaining rum.

Whip cream until just thick, and fold half into chestnut mixture.

Sandwich cake layers with some of chestnut mixture and transfer to a serving plate. Pipe or spread remaining chestnut mixture around and on top of sponge cakes.

Put remaining cream in a piping bag fitted with a small star nozzle. Decorate top of dessert with a large swirl of cream and pipe small rosettes around base.

Serves 6-8

Petits Pots au Chocolat

4 oz (110 g) dark or semisweet
  baking chocolate
2½ cups (625 mL) milk
2 eggs
2 egg yolks
3 tbsp (45 mL) granulated sugar
2 tsp (10 mL) rum
½ cup (125 mL) whipping
  cream, whipped

Preheat oven to 325°F (170°C).

Grate one square of chocolate for decoration and reserve. Place milk in a saucepan with remaining chocolate and heat to melt it.

Beat eggs, egg yolks and sugar together until light, then pour in the hot but not boiling milk, stirring all the time. Stir in rum, then strain mixture into 6 individual ovenproof dishes.

Stand dishes in a roasting pan half-filled with hot water, bake for 40-60 minutes or until custards are lightly set.

Serve hot or cold, decorated with whipped cream and grated chocolate.

Serves 6

Crêpes Tia Maria

1 cup (250 mL) all-purpose
  flour
1 tbsp (15 mL) granulated sugar
pinch of salt
2 eggs
2 egg yolks
1¼ cups (310 mL) milk
1 tbsp (15 mL) melted
  butter
3 tbsp (45 mL) Tia Maria
butter
extra Tia Maria

Blend together everything except butter and extra Tia Maria until mixture is smooth. Cover and let stand for 1 hour.

Pour a little mixture into a lightly greased pan and cook over medium heat on both sides until golden. Mixture will make 14-16 small crêpes.

To prepare crêpes, fold each crêpe into four to make a triangle. Heat a little butter and Tia Maria in a frying pan, add some folded crêpes and heat gently for a few minutes. Keep crêpes warm until served. Serve with Quick Rich Chocolate Sauce (see recipe page 11).

Note: Crêpes may be made in advance and stored in refrigerator.

Serves 4-6

Banana Boats

1¼ cups (310 mL) vanilla
  ice cream
4 bananas, peeled
3 tbsp (45 mL) chopped nuts

Chocolate Sauce

8 oz (225 g) dark or semisweet
  baking chocolate
2 cups (500 mL) water
1 tbsp (15 mL) sugar
few drops vanilla extract
¼ cup (60 mL) heavy cream
2 tsp (10 mL) butter

Prepare chocolate sauce following instructions in Pears Hélène recipe. Allow sauce to cool.

Place 2 scoops ice cream in each of 4 sundae glasses. Place a banana on top and pour chocolate sauce over. Sprinkle each serving with chopped nuts and serve immediately.

Serves 4

*Crêpes Tia Maria with Quick Rich
Chocolate Sauce (recipe page 11)*

Chocolate Walnut Pancakes

Beat batter until bubbly

Tilt pan to thinly coat bottom with batter

Loosen edges with a metal spatula

Walnut Filling

⅓ cup (85 mL) sultana
   raisins
2-3 tbsp (30-45 mL) rum
5 tbsp (75 mL) butter
1 cup (250 mL) very
   finely chopped walnuts
¾ cup (185 mL) sugar
few drops vanilla extract
¼ cup (60 mL) heavy
   cream

Chocolate Sauce

4 oz (110 g) dark or
   semisweet baking
   chocolate
2 tsp (10 mL) cornstarch
1 cup (250 mL) milk
2 tsp (10 mL) sugar
¼ cup (60 mL) cream
½ tsp (2 mL) cinnamon

Basic Pancake Batter

1 cup (250 mL) all-purpose   1 egg
   flour   1¼ cups (310 mL) milk
½ tsp (2 mL) salt   oil for frying

To make walnut filling, soak sultanas in rum for 15 minutes. Soften butter and blend in walnuts, sugar, vanilla and cream. Mix well, then add rum and raisins.

To make chocolate sauce, break chocolate into small pan and add ¼ cup (60 mL) cold water. Stir over gentle heat until melted and smooth. Blend cornstarch with a little of the milk and stir into chocolate with sugar and remaining milk. Gradually bring to a boil and simmer for 5 minutes, stirring. Remove from heat and stir in cream and cinnamon.

To make pancakes, sift flour and salt into a bowl. Add egg and half of milk and beat thoroughly until smooth. Mix in remaining milk and beat until bubbly.

Put oil for frying in a heatproof jug. Pour a little of the oil into a 6 inch (15 cm) frying pan over fairly high heat. Tilt pan to coat with oil, then pour any excess back into jug.

When pan is hot, pour in a little batter, tilting pan to thinly coat base. Cook quickly, shaking pan and loosening edge of pancake with a metal spatula until underside is golden brown. Turn pancake and cook other side.

Slide cooked pancake onto a plate and keep warm, covered with a second plate. Repeat with remaining batter, to make 8-10 pancakes.

Put a little of walnut filling onto each cooked pancake, roll up pancakes and transfer to a heated serving dish. Cover and keep warm.

Gently reheat chocolate sauce and pour over pancakes. Serve immediately.

Serves 4

Chocolate Cheesecake

Base

6 oz (170 g) chocolate or
    graham wafers
3 tbsp (45 mL) butter
1½ oz (40g) chocolate

Filling

3 medium eggs
⅓ cup (85 mL) sugar
1 large orange
½ lemon
12 oz (350 g) firm-style
    cottage cheese
1 tbsp (15 mL) gelatine
⅔ cup (165 mL) whipping
    cream
1 oz (30 g) chocolate,
    for decoration

First make base. Crush cookies finely. Melt butter and chocolate together over gentle heat. Remove from heat, stir in cookie crumbs until evenly coated in chocolate.

Press mixture into base of a 7 inch (18 cm) spring-form cake pan. Chill until firm (5 hours minimum).

To make filling, separate eggs and place yolks in a bowl with sugar. Whisk until thick and creamy. Grate rind from orange and lemon into yolk mixture. Sieve cottage cheese into mixture.

Squeeze juice from orange and lemon into small saucepan. Sprinkle gelatine over fruit juices. Allow to soften for 5 minutes. Place pan over very low heat and leave until liquid is clear, about 3 minutes. Cool slightly.

Meanwhile, beat egg and cheese mixture in bowl until smooth. Pour in cooled, dissolved gelatine and fruit juice in a thin stream, stirring all the time. Whip cream until it just holds its shape. Fold into mixture.

Whisk egg whites until stiff. Fold into cheesecake mixture using a metal spoon. Spoon filling over chocolate-cookie crumb base. Refrigerate for several hours or overnight if preferred.

When firm, unmold onto a serving plate. Melt chocolate in a bowl over hot water, and put it in a grease-proof piping bag. Drizzle chocolate in a decorative pattern over cheesecake. Allow to set before serving.

Serves 8

Chocolate Orange Cheesecake

8 oz (225 g) graham wafers
¼ lb (110 g) butter
pinch cinnamon
butter for greasing
¼ cup (60 mL) milk
3 oz (90 g) dark or
    semisweet baking
    chocolate
8 oz (225 g) cream cheese
3 tbsp (45 mL) water
1 tbsp (15 mL) powdered
    gelatine
juice and grated rind
    of 1 orange
⅔ cup (165 mL) whipping
    cream, whipped
caramelized orange rind
    (see following recipe)

Crush graham wafers. Melt butter and blend with crushed wafers and cinnamon.

Grease bottom and sides of 8-inch (20 cm) spring-form cake pan with butter and line sides with waxed paper. Spread cookie mixture over base of pan. Refrigerate while preparing filling.

Place milk and chocolate in a saucepan and heat gently, stirring until chocolate melts. Mix well with cream cheese.

Heat water and dissolve gelatine. Reheat until you have a clear, jelly-like substance.

Stir gelatine into cream cheese with orange rind and juice. Fold in whipped cream, and then pour mixture into pan.

Chill in refrigerator for 3 hours until set and firm. Remove cheesecake from pan and place on a serving plate. Decorate top with caramelized orange rind.

Serves 6-8

Caramelized Orange Rind

2 oranges, peeled in strips
¼ cup (60 mL) sugar
¼ cup (60 mL) water
3 tbsp (45 mL) Grand
    Marnier or Cointreau

Scrape pith from orange peel. Cut peel into julienne strips. Place in a saucepan and cover with cold water. Slowly bring to a boil then cover pan. Simmer 10 minutes. Drain.

Place sugar in a pan with the water. Stir over low heat until sugar dissolves. Bring to a boil and cook fairly briskly until syrup becomes tacky and thickish. Remove from heat. Cool slightly.

Stir in Grand Marnier or Cointreau. Add strips of peel to syrup. Cook gently until peel begins to look transparent. Remove peel with a slotted spoon. Cool, then use for decoration.

1 Spread crushed wafer mixture over base of springform pan

2 Stir gelatine, orange rind and juice into cream cheese mixture

3 Pour mixture into pan to set

Chocolate Orange Cheesecake

Chocolate Rum Fondue

8 oz (225 g) dark or
   semisweet baking
   chocolate
⅓ cup (85 mL) whipping
   cream
3 tbsp (45 mL) rum
3 tbsp (45 mL) orange
   juice

3 mandarin oranges,
   segmented
2 apples, cored and sliced
2 bananas, sliced
8 oz (225 g) can pineapple
   pieces, drained
½ lemon

Melt chocolate, broken into pieces, with cream, rum and orange juice in a fondue dish or a heatproof bowl over pan of hot water. Keep warm.

Arrange pieces of fruit decoratively in a bowl with small wooden forks or cocktail sticks. Squeeze lemon over fruit to preserve color.

Allow guests to dip the fruit of their choice into chocolate rum sauce. Alternatively, serve fondue with ladyfingers.

Serves 6

Divide pudding mixture between 2 bowls, add lemon to one and cocoa to the other

Chocolate Marble Pudding

1⅓ cups (335 mL)
   self-rising flour
pinch salt
¼ lb (110 g) butter
½ cup (125 mL) sugar
2 eggs, beaten

a little milk
grated rind of 1 lemon
few drops vanilla extract
3 tbsp (45 mL) cocoa
   powder
butter for greasing

Sift together flour and salt. Place butter and sugar in a mixing bowl, food processor or blender and cream until light and fluffy.

Add beaten eggs gradually, beating all the time, then fold in sifted flour, ½ at a time. Stir in a little milk so that mixture is not too stiff.

Divide mixture between 2 bowls and add lemon rind and vanilla extract to one and cocoa to the other.

Grease a 4-cup (1 L) heatproof bowl or pudding basin and add lemon and chocolate mixtures alternately, a spoonful at a time.

Cover securely with greased waxed paper, or aluminum foil, tie with string and steam for 1½-2 hours. Serve pudding very hot with chocolate sauce.

Note: You can use other flavorings and colorings to make a marble pudding. Try adding coffee extract, or grated orange rind and orange juice to achieve different effects and flavors. Always add the different colored mixtures in spoonfuls to get an attractive marbled effect.

Serves 6

Chocolate Marble Pudding

Add mixtures alternately to heatproof bowl

Cover securely with aluminum foil

SOUFFLÉS

Orange and Chocolate Soufflé

oil for greasing
⅓ cup (85 mL) cocoa powder
1¾ cups (440 mL) milk
3 large eggs, separated
finely grated rind and
   juice of 1 orange
⅓ cup (85 mL) sugar
1 tbsp (15 mL) powdered
   gelatine
¼ cup (50 mL) hot water
1¼ cups (310 mL) whipping
   cream
2 oz (60 g) dark or baking
   chocolate, grated

Place a double band of waxed paper around a 3½-cup (875 mL) soufflé dish to come 2 inches (5 cm) above rim, and tie it securely with string. Very lightly grease dish and waxed paper.

Place cocoa with milk in a pan. Bring to a boil, stirring. Blend egg yolks with orange rind, juice and sugar and stir in chocolate milk. Return mixture to pan and stir over gentle heat until custard thickens. Remove from heat.

Dissolve gelatine in ¼ cup (60 mL) hot water. Mix with custard, then cool quickly until just beginning to set.

Whip half the cream until just thick. Whisk egg whites until stiff, but not dry. Fold cream into custard, then fold in egg whites. Transfer mixture to prepared soufflé dish. Leave to set completely.

Remove paper band from the set soufflé. Press grated chocolate around exposed sides of soufflé. Whip the remaining cream and pipe on top, decorate with chocolate curls.

Serves 6

Place double band of waxed paper around soufflé dish, and tie securely

Stir egg mixture into chocolate milk

Fold egg whites into cool custard mixture

Chocolate Rum Soufflé

1¾ cups (440 mL) milk
5 tbsp (75 mL) cocoa
  powder
⅓ cup (85 mL) sugar
3 large eggs, separated
2 tsp (10 mL) rum
⅔ cup (165 mL) whipping
  cream

⅓ cup (85 mL) warm
  water
2 tbsp (30 mL) powdered
  gelatine
2 oz (60 g) chocolate curls
  or caraque (see recipe)

Fold a doubled sheet of waxed paper around a soufflé dish of 3-cup (750 mL) capacity, so that paper reaches at least 2 inches (5 cm) above rim, and tie it in place with string. Lightly grease inside of dish and waxed paper.

Blend milk and cocoa in a pan and bring to a boil, stirring. In a bowl, cream sugar, egg yolks and rum together. Gradually pour in the chocolate milk, stirring. Return mixture to pan and heat gently without boiling, stirring constantly, until it thickens. Allow to cool a little.

Beat cream until thick and stir into custard. Dissolve gelatine in water and add it to the half-cooled custard. Leave custard in a cool place until almost on the point of setting.

In a clean bowl, beat egg whites until stiff. Fold them into chocolate custard and pour mixture into prepared soufflé dish. Leave in a cool place or refrigerator until set.

Undo string and remove paper by holding a knife alongside soufflé dish and peeling paper carefully away. Sprinkle edge of soufflé with chocolate curls or caraque. Serve at once.

Note: Vary this recipe by adding liqueur of your choice instead of rum.

Serves 6

Viennese Soufflé

A classic chocolate soufflé from Vienna – served cold with lavish amounts of whipped cream and guaranteed not to let the cook down.

8 oz (225 g) baking
  chocolate
½ tsp (2.5 mL) instant
  coffee
3 tbsp (45 mL) Grand
  Marnier
6 large eggs

¾ cup (185 mL) sugar
¾ cup (185 mL) butter,
  softened
pinch of salt or cream
  of tartar
⅔ cup (165 mL) whipping
  cream for serving

Whipped Cream Topping

⅔ cup (165 mL) whipping
  cream

3 tbsp (45 mL) sherry

Break chocolate into a heatproof bowl.

Dissolve coffee in ¼ cup (60 mL) hot water and add to chocolate. Add Grand Marnier.

Place bowl over a pan of hot water on very low heat. Stir until chocolate has melted. Set aside.

Separate eggs, placing whites in a large clean bowl and yolks in a small bowl. Beat yolks with sugar and butter until creamy. Stir into melted chocolate. Leave until mixture has cooled.

Whisk egg whites with salt or cream of tartar until very stiff. Fold in chocolate mixture.

Butter a 7-cup (1.75 L) deep heatproof bowl or pudding bowl. Pour in mixture and make a slight hollow in center with the back of a spoon. Cover top of mold tightly with foil.

Place bowl in a pan with water reaching halfway up the sides. Bring water to a boil, cover pan and let steam for 1½ hours. Top up with extra water during cooking if necessary. When soufflé is firm, remove from pan and leave to cool.

Unmold onto a serving plate. Whip cream until thick, add sherry and pour over soufflé. Serve with additional cream, if desired.

Serves 6

Hot Chocolate Soufflé

4 oz (110 g) dark or
  baking chocolate
3 tbsp (45 mL) water
1¼ cups (310 mL) milk
¼ cup (60 mL) sugar
2-3 drops vanilla extract

1 tbsp (15 mL) all-
  purpose flour
2 tsp (10 mL) arrowroot
2 tbsp (30 mL) butter
3 egg yolks
4 egg whites

Preheat oven to 325°F (170°C). Prepare a soufflé dish as for Orange and Chocolate Soufflé (see recipe previous page).

Break chocolate into a heatproof bowl, add water and stir over gentle heat until melted. Reserve 5 tbsp (75 mL) of milk and add remainder to melted chocolate. Bring to a boil and add sugar and vanilla extract.

Blend reserved milk with flour and arrowroot, stir into chocolate and bring to a boil, stirring continuously. Boil for 2 seconds, remove from heat and dot the surface with the butter. Cover and let custard stand for 5 minutes.

Beat egg yolks into custard one at a time.

Stiffly beat egg whites and fold into custard. Turn into soufflé dish and bake for 45 minutes. Remove from oven, undo string and remove paper by holding a knife alongside soufflé dish and peeling paper carefully away. Serve immediately.

Serves 4

Chocolate Chestnut Ring (recipe next page)

PASTRY
AND CHOCOLATE

Chocolate Chestnut Ring

½ quantity Choux Pastry
(see recipe next page)

Filling and Icing

6 oz (170 g) semisweet
  baking chocolate
3 tbsp (45 mL) water
3 tbsp (45 mL) rum
3 tbsp (45 mL) butter

1¼ cups (310 mL) cream,
  whipped
16 oz (450 g) chestnut purée
½ cup (125 mL) icing
  sugar

Preheat oven to 400°F (200°C).

Spoon choux pastry into a 10 inch (25 cm) circle on a greased baking sheet.

Bake on middle shelf of oven for 45-50 minutes, until well risen and crisp. Remove from oven. Make a few small slits in sides to allow steam to escape. Return to oven for 5 minutes to dry out, then cool. Cut in half horizontally, and scoop out any uncooked pastry.

About 1 hour before serving, heat chocolate and water in saucepan. When chocolate melts, stir in rum and butter. Cool until chocolate begins to thicken.

Whip cream until thick.

Put bottom half of choux pastry ring on a rack over a plate.

Beat chestnut purée with icing sugar until smooth. Fill ring with chestnut purée mixture. Pipe or spoon whipped cream on top. Replace top half of ring. Carefully spread chocolate icing over top. Remove to a dish. Chill and serve.

Note: These choux pastry shells can also be filled with soft fruit such as peaches, raspberries, strawberries or black currants. Process or sieve the fruit with sugar to make a purée, fold into the whipped cream and use instead of chestnut filling.

Serves 8 (pictured on previous page)

Profiteroles with Rum Sauce

½ quantity Choux Pastry
(see recipe next page)
1¼ cups (310 mL)
  whipping cream,
  whipped
1 tbsp (15 mL) sugar

Sauce

8 oz (225 g) semisweet
  baking chocolate
¼ cup (60 mL) rum
3 tbsp (45 mL) butter

Preheat oven to 400°F (200°C).

On a greased baking sheet, put 18 heaped teaspoonfuls, well separated, of Choux Pastry. Bake for 20 minutes until well risen and golden brown. Remove from oven, make a small slit in side of each to allow steam to escape. Return to oven for 5 minutes to dry out, then cool.

Just before serving, whip cream with sugar until stiff. Using a piping bag, fill each profiterole through side slit and pile them on a dish.

To make sauce, melt chocolate and rum in bowl over pan of boiling water. Add butter and mix well. Pour over profiteroles and serve cold.

Makes 18

Chocolate Almond Cream Flan

¾ cup (185 mL) margarine
½ cup (125 mL) icing sugar
¼ cup (60 mL) cocoa powder
1 egg, beaten
2½ cups (625 mL) all-purpose
  flour
1 oz (30 g) grated chocolate
  or caraque (see recipe)

Almond Cream

1¼ cups (310 mL) milk
¼ cup (60 mL) ground
  almonds
¼ cup (60 mL) sugar
⅓ cup (85 mL) heavy cream
¼ cup (60 mL) cornstarch

Preheat oven to 375°F (190°C).

Cream margarine and sugar together. Beat in cocoa and egg. Blend in flour gradually and knead to a smooth dough. Let stand for 30 minutes.

Lightly grease an 8 inch (20 cm) flan or quiche pan. Roll out pastry to ¼ inch (0.5 cm) thick and line pan. Prick pastry base. Bake blind (lined with foil and weighted with dried beans) for 25 minutes. Allow to cool.

Meanwhile, bring milk to a boil. Remove from heat. Stir in ground almonds, sugar, cream and cornstarch to make smooth, thick mixture. Heat gently, stirring, for 3-4 minutes until well thickened. Allow to cool and pour into flan shell. Chill until set. Sprinkle with grated chocolate or caraque (page 72), decorate with toffee almonds (see note), and serve.

Note: To make toffee almonds, put ½ cup (125 mL) sugar in small saucepan. Add 3-4 tbsp (45-60 mL) water, dissolve and boil until mixture turns golden. Quickly drop almonds into it, coat them with toffee, lift out with teaspoon and drop on greased flat surface to set.

Serves 6

Chocolate and Coffee Éclairs

¾ quantity Choux Pastry
(see following recipe)

Cream Filling

4 egg yolks
½ cup (125 mL) sugar
5 tbsp (75 mL) cornstarch
3 cups (750 mL) milk
1 tbsp (15 mL) cocoa powder
1 tbsp (15 mL) instant coffee

Icing

2 cups (500 mL) icing
   sugar
5 tbsp (75 mL) hot water
1 tbsp (15 mL) cocoa
   powder or melted
   dark chocolate
1 tbsp (15 mL) instant
   coffee

Preheat oven to 400°F (200°C).

Using a piping bag, pipe the Choux Pastry into 12 equal lengths. Bake for 20 minutes, then cool. To make filling, beat egg yolks, sugar and cornstarch in a saucepan. Heat milk, pour onto egg mixture and stir over heat until it thickens. Cool and divide in half. Flavor one half with cocoa mixed to a paste with a little water, and the other with coffee powder, dissolved in a little boiling water.

Mix sifted icing sugar with hot water. Flavor half with cocoa or chocolate and half with coffee powder.

Just before serving, carefully split éclairs open (without separating halves) and fill one half of each éclair with chocolate filling and the other half with coffee filling.

Coat éclairs with icing, half chocolate and half coffee, and decorate with whipped cream.

Makes 12

Choux Pastry

1¼ cups (310 mL) water
2 tsp (10 mL) sugar
¼ lb (110 g) butter
2 cups (500 mL) all-purpose
   flour, sifted
pinch salt
5-6 eggs, beaten

Preheat oven to 400°F (200°C).

In a large saucepan, bring water, sugar and butter to a boil. Remove from heat immediately.

Add sifted flour and salt. Mix in well. Return pan to the heat and stir continuously until mixture leaves sides of pan. Remove from heat and let cool.

Gradually add beaten eggs, mixing well, until paste is of a dropping consistency. Place in a piping bag fitted with a plain nozzle. It is now ready to use.

Makes approximately 2 lbs (1 kg)

Chocolate Egg Nog Pie

1⅓ cups (335 mL) all-purpose
   flour
¼ cup (60 mL) chocolate
   milk powder
¼ lb (110 g) butter or
   margarine
2 tbsp (30 mL) cold water

Filling

⅓ cup (85 mL) sugar
2 eggs
¼ cup (60 mL) all-purpose
   flour
1¼ cups (310 mL) milk
1 tsp (5 mL) vanilla extract
⅔ cup (165 mL) whipping
   cream
1 tbsp (15 mL) rum
grated nutmeg

Preheat oven to 400°F (200°C). Sift together flour and chocolate powder and add margarine or butter, cut into pieces. Cut in until mixture resembles fine breadcrumbs. Mix to a firm dough with water.

Knead dough lightly and roll out to fit an 8 inch (20 cm) fluted pie plate or quiche pan. Bake blind (lined with foil weighted with dried beans) for 20 minutes.

To make filling: Place ¼ cup (60 mL) sugar in a bowl with 1 egg and 1 egg yolk. Beat well and mix in flour. Warm milk with vanilla extract and pour onto egg mixture, stirring. Return to milk pan and stir over gentle heat until thickened. Cool slightly. Pour into flan shell, let cool then chill.

Beat remaining egg white until stiff and peaking, then whisk in remaining sugar. Whip cream with rum and fold gently into egg white. Spread mixture over custard filling and sprinkle with nutmeg.

Serves 6

Chocolate Meringue Pie

1 sweet shortcrust pie crust, (see following recipe)
7 oz (200 g) melted semisweet chocolate
1 tbsp (15 mL) gelatine
3 tbsp (45 mL) water
½ cup (125 mL) cornstarch
1 cup (250 mL) sugar
3½ cups (875 mL) milk
¼ cup (60 mL) butter
6 egg yolks
few drops vanilla extract

Meringue

3 egg whites
⅓ cup (85 mL) sugar

Preheat oven to 400°F (200°C). Prepare a 9 inch (23 cm) pastry shell and bake it blind (lined with foil, weighted with dried beans). Let it cool.

In a bowl, melt chocolate over simmering water. Dissolve gelatine in water. Blend together cornstarch and sugar. Warm milk and add gradually to cornstarch mixture. Add melted chocolate and dissolved gelatine. Return mixture to pan and cook, stirring over gentle heat until it thickens.

Remove pan from heat. Stir in butter and egg yolks and flavor with vanilla extract. Allow to cool slightly. Pour mixture into pie crust. Refrigerate until set.

In another bowl, beat egg whites until stiff. Gradually add sugar. Spoon meringue over chocolate filling. Bake for about 15 minutes until meringue is crisp and golden on top. If meringue browns too quickly, open door slightly for 1 minute and reduce temperature to 350°F (180°C) for remainder of cooking.

Cool before serving.

Serves 6

Sweet Shortcrust Pastry

Sufficient for ½ lb (225 g) pastry.

2 cups (500 mL) all-purpose flour
pinch salt
¼ lb (110 g) butter
¼ cup (60 mL) sugar
1 egg yolk
2 tsp (10 mL) lemon juice
2-3 tbsp (30-45 mL) cold water

Sift flour and salt into a large bowl. Add butter and cut it in until mixture resembles fine breadcrumbs. Add sugar and mix.

Make a well in the center of mixture. Add egg yolk, lemon juice and water. Mix to a slightly crumbly, stiff dough. Knead lightly.

Cover with plastic wrap and chill 30 minutes before using.

Chocolate Meringue Pie

CHOCOLATE CAKES AND COOKIES

Chocolate Deluxe

This cake should be filled at least 2-3 hours before serving. It can be made the day before and kept in the refrigerator overnight. This will ensure that the meringue is soft enough to cut.

4 egg whites
1 cup (250 mL) sugar
9 oz (250 g) dark or
　semisweet baking
　chocolate
½ cup (125 mL) water
2½ cups (625 mL)
　whipping cream
2 oz (60 g) caraque
　(see recipe page 72)

Preheat oven to 250°F (130°C). Line 3 baking sheets with nonstick parchment paper and mark three 8-9 inch (20-23 cm) circles on the paper.

Beat egg whites until stiff, add half the sugar and beat until stiff and glossy. Fold in remaining sugar. Spread mixture over marked circles and bake for about 1 hour, until dry.

Break chocolate into small pieces and place in a small pan with water. Melt over gentle heat, then cool.

Whip cream until it begins to thicken, then add cool chocolate mixture and continue to beat until thick.

Spread each meringue round with chocolate cream and layer one on top of the other. Spread top and sides with mixture, and let stand 2-3 hours. Decorate cake with additional piped chocolate mixture, and drizzle melted chocolate on top.

Serves 6-8

Spread meringue mixture in circles

Add cooled chocolate mixture to whipped cream

Spread each meringue with chocolate cream

Lamington Squares

Base

¾ cup (185 mL) butter
¾ cup (185 mL) sugar
3 eggs, beaten
2 cups (500 mL) self-
  rising flour

⅔ cup (165 mL) milk
½ tsp (2 mL) vanilla
  extract

Icing

2 tbsp (30 mL) butter
¼ cup (60 mL) boiling
  water
3 tbsp (45 mL) cocoa
  powder

2¾ cups (685 mL) icing
  sugar
2 cups (500 mL) shredded
  coconut

Two days before you plan to serve these, make the cake base. Preheat oven to 350°F (180°C).

Cream butter and sugar until light and fluffy. Gradually add beaten eggs, beating well after each addition. Alternately fold in flour and milk, then stir in vanilla extract.

Place mixture in greased, lined jelly roll pan and bake for 30-35 minutes. Cool cake on wire rack. Let stand for 2 days, then cut cake into 1½ inch (3.5 cm) cubes.

To prepare icing: Place butter in a bowl and pour in boiling water. Add cocoa and, beating continuously, gradually add icing sugar. Place bowl of icing over pan of hot water. Using a long-pronged fork to hold cubes of cake, dip each piece into icing and roll immediately in coconut. Leave squares to set.

Makes approximately 24

Chocolate Glaze Icing

1¼ cups (310 mL) icing
  sugar
1 tbsp (15 mL) cocoa
  powder

1 tbsp (15 mL) boiling
  water
1 tsp (5 mL) butter

Sift icing sugar and cocoa powder into small heatproof bowl. Melt butter in boiling water then add to icing sugar mixture, stirring well to make smooth paste. Place bowl over a saucepan of boiling water and stir mixture for 1 minute.

Pour icing over cake and smooth surface with spatula or knife dipped in hot water.

Note: To make plain glaze icing, omit cocoa powder and butter. To make coffee glaze icing, add 1 tbsp (15 mL) instant coffee instead of cocoa powder.

Makes enough to cover an 8 inch (20 cm) cake

Chocolate Butter Icing

1½ cups (375 mL) icing
  sugar
1 tbsp (15 mL) cocoa
  powder

¼ lb (110 g) butter
1 tbsp (15 mL) sherry
few drops vanilla extract

Sift icing sugar with cocoa powder. Beat butter until light and creamy. Gradually beat in half the icing sugar. Beat in sherry alternately with remaining sugar. Stir in vanilla extract.

Makes enough to fill or top an 8 inch (20 cm) cake

Chocolate Chestnut Cake

¼ lb (110 g) plus 1 tbsp
  (15 mL) margarine
  or butter
½ cup (125 mL) sugar
2 eggs, beaten
1 cup (250 mL) self-rising
  flour

¼ cup (60 mL) cocoa
  powder
16 oz (450 g) canned
  chestnut purée
1 tbsp (15 mL) rum
½ cup (125 mL) icing
  sugar

Icing

4 oz (110 g) dark or
  semisweet baking
  chocolate
¼ cup (60 mL) water

1 tsp (5 mL) unflavored
  vegetable oil
3 tbsp (45 mL) sugar

Preheat oven to 375°F (190°C). Grease an 8 inch (20 cm) cake pan and line with waxed paper.

Cream margarine or butter with sugar until light and fluffy. Add eggs gradually, beating all the time. Sift together flour and cocoa powder and gradually fold them into mixture. Place in cake pan and bake for 20-25 minutes until well risen and browned on top. Cool on rack.

Cut cake into three equal layers horizontally. In a bowl, beat together chestnut purée, rum and icing sugar. Spread mixture on 2 lower layers of cake, and sandwich all layers together.

In a pan over low heat, melt together chocolate, water, oil and sugar. Stir well to blend thoroughly. Allow to cool until quite thick, but not set. Pour chocolate mixture over cake. Leave in a cool place to set before serving.

Note: Cake can be decorated with chocolate leaves. Melt dark chocolate in top of double boiler. Allow to cool slightly. Using small teaspoon or spatula, carefully spread chocolate on undersides of washed and dried firm leaves (e.g. camellias, orange). Allow to set at room temperature. Carefully peel leaf from chocolate, starting at stem end.

Serves 6-8

Chocolate Log

3 eggs
½ cup (125 mL) sugar
1 cup (250 mL) all-purpose
    flour
1 tbsp (15 mL) hot water
5 tbsp (75 mL) apricot jam
¼ lb (110 g) softened butter
1⅓ cups (335 mL) icing
    sugar
3-4 tbsp (45-60 mL) warm
    milk
2 oz (60 g) chocolate,
    melted

Fold half the flour into egg mixture

Preheat oven to 425°F (220°C). Line a 9 by 13 inch (22 by 33 cm) jelly roll pan with waxed paper.

Place eggs and sugar in a large heatproof bowl and whisk over pan of hot water until light and creamy. Remove bowl from heat and whisk until cool. Alternatively, beat eggs and sugar with an electric mixer until light and creamy.

Sift flour and gently fold half of it into mixture, using a metal spoon. Fold in rest of flour and stir in hot water.

Pour mixture into lined jelly roll pan so that it is completely covered and bake for 7-9 minutes until cooked and golden brown.

While cake is cooking, lay a large sheet of waxed paper on a damp dishcloth and sprinkle with white sugar. Warm the apricot jam.

As soon as cake is cooked, turn it out on the sugared paper and peel off lining paper. Trim edges neatly and spread the whole surface with warmed jam. Roll up from one of the long edges with the aid of the sugared paper.

Diagonally slice across 1 end of roll, and place slice on top of roll to form a 'knob'. Place cake on cake board or serving plate.

Cream butter until soft. Beat in icing sugar a little at a time. Add sufficient milk to make a spreading consistency.

Mix buttercream with melted chocolate and spread evenly over top, sides and ends of cake to completely cover it. Run a fork along top and sides to make horizontal grooves.

Place a little melted chocolate in a piping bag and pipe 3 or 4 concentric circles on 'knob' and ends of log to resemble rings on a tree trunk.

Serves 6

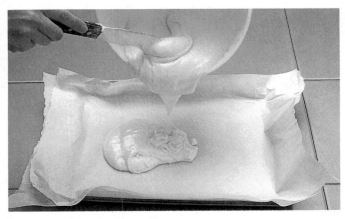

Pour into lined jelly roll pan

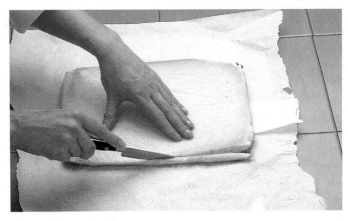

Trim edges of cake

Chocolate Petits Fours

8 oz (225 g) dark or
   semisweet baking
   chocolate
¼ lb (110 g) margarine
   or butter
½ cup (125 mL) sugar
2 eggs
1 cup (250 mL) self-rising
   flour
fat for greasing
¼ cup (60 mL) strawberry
   jam
1 tbsp (15 mL) curaçao
½ cup (125 mL) whipping
   cream
12 strawberries

Melt chocolate in a bowl set over pan of hot water. Spread chocolate on 2 sheets of waxed paper, to make level rectangles of 8 x 12 inches (20 by 30 cm). Leave to set. Cut each sheet of chocolate into 24 squares, 2 inches (5 cm) square, using hot, wet knife.

Preheat oven to 375°F (190°C).

In a bowl, cream margarine or butter with sugar until light and fluffy. Beat in eggs and then gradually fold in sifted flour.

Grease a 9 by 13 inch (22 by 33 cm) baking pan and line base with waxed paper. Spread cake mixture into pan and bake for about 20 minutes. Cool on a wire rack.

Cut cake in half crosswise and trim each piece to a rectangle measuring 6 x 8 inches (15 x 20 cm). Sandwich the 2 pieces of cake with half the strawberry jam. Sprinkle with curaçao.

Cut cake rectangle into 12 squares, each 2 x 2 inches (5 x 5 cm). Spread rest of jam thinly on sides of cake squares. Stick a chocolate square onto each of the 4 sides of the cakes.

Whip cream until stiff and pipe a swirl of cream on top of each chocolate petits fours. Wash strawberries and place one on top of each cake.

Note: Chocolate petits fours can be varied with other flavors. For example, fill with a layer of cherry jam, sprinkle with kirsch, and top with a fresh cherry; or fill with marmalade, sprinkle with Grand Marnier and top with an orange slice or candied orange peel.

Makes 12

Sacher Torte

9 oz (250 g) semisweet
  chocolate
⅔ cup (165 mL) butter
⅔ cup (165 mL) sugar
6 eggs, separated
1¼ cups (310 mL) self-
  rising flour
3 tbsp (45 mL) apricot jam
a little coffee glaze icing
  (see glaze icing recipe)

Coating

7 oz (200 g) semisweet
  chocolate
3 tbsp (45 mL) copha fat
  or vegetable shortening

Preheat oven to 350°F (180°C). Break chocolate into squares and place in bowl over a pan of hot but not boiling water, over low heat. Leave to soften, but do not melt.

Blend softened chocolate and butter with a wooden spoon. Add sugar and mix well.

Beat in egg yolks, one at a time, and beat until blended.

In another bowl, beat egg whites until stiff. Fold egg whites and flour alternately into chocolate mixture, finishing with egg white. Be careful not to overmix or beat the mixture.

Pour mixture into 2 greased and floured 8 inch (20 cm) round cake pans. Bake for 45-60 minutes until well risen. Leave in pans overnight.

The following day, turn out cakes. Boil jam for a few minutes and spread over each cake. Sandwich cake halves together.

To make covering, break chocolate into bowl and melt with copha over pan of hot water. Stir gently until dissolved, then spread to completely cover cake. Allow to set.

Decorate with the words 'Sacher Torte' piped in coffee-flavored buttercream, if desired.

Serves 6-8

Sacher Torte

Marble Cake

fat for greasing
¾ cup (185 mL) margarine
    or butter
¾ cup (185 mL) sugar
3 large eggs
1¼ cups (310 mL)
    all-purpose flour
¾ cup (185 mL)
    self-rising flour
1 tbsp (15 mL) cocoa
    powder
a little milk
chocolate, orange and
    yellow food colorings
finely grated rind of
    1 orange
1 tsp (5 mL) orange juice
finely grated rind of
    1 lemon
1 tsp (5 mL) lemon juice
few drops vanilla extract

Preheat oven to 325°F (170°C). Grease an 8 inch (20 cm) tube pan, line it with waxed paper and re-grease.

Place the margarine or butter and sugar in a mixer bowl and, with mixer at high speed, cream mixture until light and fluffy. Add eggs, one at a time, beating well. Sift flours together and fold into mixture with large metal spoon.

Divide mixture into 4 portions. Mix cocoa powder, 1 tsp (5 mL) milk and a few drops of chocolate coloring into one portion. Add orange rind and juice to second portion, with a few drops of orange coloring. Add lemon rind and juice to third portion with a few drops of yellow coloring. Add vanilla to last portion.

Place spoonfuls of mixtures alternately in prepared cake pan. Bake for 45-55 minutes until cake is well risen and firm to the touch. Remove from oven and allow cake to cool slightly. Turn out on a wire rack to complete cooling.

Serves 8

Chocolate Layer Cake

½ cup (125 mL) butter
½ cup (125 mL) sugar
1½ tbsp (20 mL) cocoa
    powder dissolved in
    2½ tbsp (40 mL)
    boiling water
2 large eggs
few drops vanilla extract
⅞ cup (220 mL) self-rising
    flour, sifted
1¼ cups (310 mL)
    whipping cream

Decoration

3 tbsp (45 mL) butter
½ cup (125 mL) icing sugar
1 tsp (5 mL) cocoa powder
½ tsp (2 mL) boiling water

Cream butter and sugar together for 5 minutes until light and creamy. Stir in cocoa liquid.

Preheat oven to 375°F (190°C). Lightly beat together eggs and vanilla extract. Add eggs to creamed mixture a little at a time, beating well after each addition. Add a little sifted flour with the last addition of egg. Using a metal spoon, fold in remaining flour.

Spoon mixture into 2 greased and lined 7 inch (18 cm) cake pans and bake on middle shelf of oven for 20-25 minutes. Turn cakes out on a rack to cool.

While cakes cool, whip cream until it forms peaks. Sandwich cake with half whipped cream and spread rest over top.

To prepare decoration: Cream together butter and icing sugar until light and fluffy. Dissolve cocoa in water and blend it with buttercream. Fit a piping bag with a small plain icing nozzle and fill with chocolate buttercream. Pipe in parallel lines over top of cake.

Note: To make chocolate walnut cake, add chopped walnuts to cake mixture. Mix ½ cup (125 mL) chopped walnuts with beaten eggs (omit vanilla extract) before beating it into creamed butter and sugar. Decorate top of cake with walnut halves or grated chocolate instead of piped chocolate buttercream.

Serves 6-8

Pear and Chocolate Sponge Cake

¾ cup (185 mL) butter or
    margarine
¾ cup (185 mL) sugar
3 eggs
1½ cups (375 mL)
    self-rising flour
5 tbsp (75 mL) chopped
    walnuts
12 canned pear halves,
    drained
7 walnut halves

Chocolate Buttercream

2 cups (500 mL) icing
    sugar
½ lb (225 g) butter
4 tsp (20 mL) cocoa
    powder
few drops vanilla extract

Preheat oven to 375°F (190°C).

Cream butter and sugar until light and fluffy, then beat in eggs, one at a time, adding a spoonful of flour with each. Sift remaining flour and fold in with a metal spoon.

Divide mixture between two greased and lined 8 inch (20 cm) square cake pans. Bake for 25-30 minutes. Turn out and cool on a wire rack.

To make chocolate buttercream: Sift icing sugar and beat with butter until light and fluffy. Blend cocoa powder with a little boiling water, and stir into butter and sugar with a few drops of vanilla extract.

Split each cake layer in half. Spread 3 layers with ½ the buttercream. Slice 6 pears and lay on top of buttercream. Sandwich together with the plain layer on top.

Spread top and sides of cake with buttercream. Press chopped nuts onto sides. Arrange remaining 6 pears over top and drizzle with chocolate. Decorate with walnut halves.

Serves 8

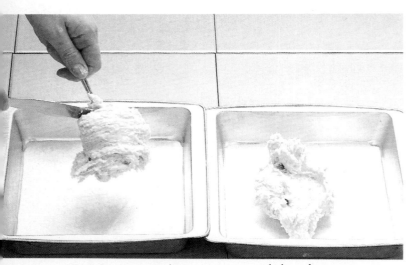

Sift flour and fold in with metal spoon

Divide mixture between greased, lined pans

Blend cocoa with a little boiling water
and stir into the butter and sugar

Vienna Cake

1½ cups (375 mL)
   all-purpose flour
1 tsp (5 mL) baking
   powder
½ tsp (2 mL) baking
   soda
½ cup (125 mL) cocoa
   powder

¼ lb (110 g) butter
1⅓ cup (335 mL) packed
   soft dark brown sugar
2 eggs
⅓ cup (85 mL) yogurt

Icing and Filling

¼ lb (110 g) butter
1 cup (250 mL) icing sugar
few drops vanilla extract
2 tsp (10 mL) cocoa
   powder
1 tbsp (15 mL) rum
⅔ cup (165 mL) whipping
   cream
8 thin chocolate triangles

Preheat oven to 375°F (190°C). Sift together flour, baking powder and baking soda. Mix cocoa with a little hot water to form a smooth paste.

In a bowl, cream butter and sugar until light and fluffy. Beat in eggs, yogurt, cocoa paste and, finally, flour mixture. Pour into a greased 8 inch (20 cm) square cake pan, the base of which is lined with waxed paper. Bake for 35 minutes. Cool on a wire rack.

Meanwhile, make the icing: Beat butter with icing sugar and vanilla extract until very light and fluffy. Fold in cocoa and rum.

In another bowl, beat the cream until stiff. When cake is cold, cut it into 3 horizontal layers, and sandwich together with whipped cream. Spread chocolate buttercream on top and decorate with chocolate triangles.

Serves 8

Chocolate Chip Cookies

¼ lb (110 g) butter
¼ cup (60 mL) sugar
½ cup (125 mL) brown
   sugar
1 egg
1 cup (250 mL)
   all-purpose flour
1 cup (250 mL) self-
   rising flour

½ tsp (2 mL) salt
½ tsp (2 mL) baking
   soda
grated rind of 1 orange
¾ cup (185 mL) chocolate
   chips or chocolate drops
½ cup (125 mL) chopped
   walnuts

Preheat oven to 375°F (190°C).
Cream butter, sugar and brown sugar together until light and fluffy. Add egg and beat thoroughly.
Sift flour, salt and baking soda into mixture and beat. Stir in orange rind, chocolate chips or drops, and nuts.
Grease baking sheet. Roll teaspoonfuls of mixture into balls, place on baking sheet and press with a fork.
Bake for about 10 minutes until golden brown. Cool and serve.

Makes about 48

Chocolate Delights

12 oz (340 g) dark or semisweet baking chocolate
1¼ cups (310 mL) whipping cream

grated rind of 1 orange
½ cup (125 mL) cocoa powder

Grate chocolate. Place cream in a small pan and bring to a boil. Tip in grated chocolate and stir well over gentle heat until it is completely melted and forms a smooth paste. Remove from heat.

Continue to stir until cooled. Stir in grated orange rind, then leave in a cool place (preferably not the refrigerator) for 24 hours.

Pour cocoa onto a plate and, using 2 small spoons, scoop out small amounts of chocolate cream and roll into smooth balls. Dip each ball in cocoa and serve immediately – do not keep too long or cream will turn sour.

Makes 1¼ lbs (560 g)

back: Chocolate Viennese, Toscanas, Chocolate Fudgies; front: Chocolate Delights, Chocolate Chip Cookies

Chocolate Fudgies

½ cup (125 mL) butter
1¾ cups (435 mL) brown
   sugar
2 eggs
1¼ cups (310 mL)
   all-purpose flour, sifted
4-5 tbsp (60-75 mL) cocoa
   powder, sifted
few drops vanilla extract
1 cup (250 mL) walnuts,
   chopped
3 tbsp (45 mL) icing sugar

Preheat oven to 350°F (180°C).

In a large bowl, cream butter and beat in sugar until light and fluffy. Add eggs, one at a time, beating continuously.

Fold in sifted flour and cocoa powder, then add vanilla and chopped nuts. Continue to mix until thoroughly blended.

Drop teaspoonfuls of mixture on greased baking sheet. Dust with icing sugar. Bake for about 12 minutes. Cool on wire rack and serve.

Makes about 48 (pictured on previous page)

Lucernes

2 oz (60 g) dark or
   baking chocolate
2 cups (500 mL) self-
   rising flour, sifted

½ cup (125 mL) soft
   margarine
1 cup (250 mL) sugar
4 eggs, beaten

Filling

1¾ cups (440 mL)
   whipping cream,
   whipped
1 tbsp (15 mL) powdered
   gelatine

few glacé cherries, halved
   or chopped

Decoration

1¼ cups (310 mL)
   whipping cream
chopped walnuts, slivered
   almonds or grated
   chocolate

Preheat oven to 400°F (200°C). Grease, line with waxed paper and grease again two 9 by 13 inch (23 by 33 cm) jelly roll pans. Melt chocolate in double boiler.

Place all other ingredients for sponge cake together in a large mixing bowl and beat well for 4-5 minutes until thoroughly blended and creamy. Add melted chocolate and mix in. Spread mixture smoothly in pans.

Bake in preheated oven for 10-12 minutes until cooked. Turn out and cool on a wire rack.

Trim hard edges neatly from cooled cakes and level them with sharp knife. Cut one cake in half lengthwise. Reserve one half and cut remaining half into 2 lengthwise, one of which should be twice as wide as the other (2:1). You should now have 3 cut cake layers, each a little narrower than the last, and one whole cake layer.

To make filling: Whip cream until it is fairly thick. Soften gelatine in a little cold water, then dissolve over a saucepan of hot water. Cool, then add to cream and whip until stiff. Fold in glacé cherries.

Spread the cut cake layers with cream mixture. Arrange layers starting with the largest at the bottom. Pile more whipped cream mixture on top and trim edges to form smooth-sided triangular shape.

Cut reserved whole cake layer in half lengthwise. Lightly score one side of each piece lengthwise with a knife. Turn over and spread unscored side with remaining cream filling. Place these two strips, filling-side down, on either side of the long layered triangle to enclose filling. The two sides should meet in a point at the top, and rest on the jutting-out base of the layered triangle.

Whip cream for decoration until stiff and spread it over outer long sides. Sprinkle sides with chopped nuts or grated chocolate. Slice crosswise into 12 equal slices.

Note: For variety, you can flavor lucernes with orange or lemon juice and grated rind, or try a few drops of peppermint extract and green food coloring.

Makes about 12 slices

Chocolate Viennese

1¼ cups (310 mL) butter
⅓ cup (85 mL) sugar
2 oz (60 g) dark or
  baking chocolate,
  melted
2¼ cups (560 mL)
  all-purpose flour

5 tbsp (75 mL) cocoa
  powder
½ cup (125 mL) ground
  almonds

Filling

¼ cup (60 mL) margarine
  or butter
½ cup (125 mL) icing
  sugar

1 tsp (5 mL) cocoa powder
2 oz (60 g) plain chocolate,
  melted

Preheat oven to 350°F (180°C). Cream butter, sugar and melted chocolate.

Sift together flour and cocoa powder and fold into mixture with ground almonds. Transfer mixture to a piping bag fitted with a ½ inch (1 cm) star nozzle and pipe 20 whirls and 20 fingers onto a greased baking sheet.

This is a very stiff mixture so extra pressure is needed to pipe it.

Bake for 10-15 minutes. Cool on a wire rack.

To make filling: Cream margarine or butter with sugar until light. Blend cocoa with a little boiling water and mix with creamed mixture. Use to sandwich whirls or fingers in pairs.

Melt chocolate in a bowl over simmering water, cool slightly. Place in a small plastic bag, snip one corner and squeeze chocolate over cookies in a decorative pattern.

Makes 20 (pictured on previous page)

Toscanas

1 cup (250 mL) self-rising
  flour
1 cup (250 mL) ground
  almonds
½ cup (125 mL) brown
  sugar

¼ lb (110 g) butter, melted
2½ oz (70 g) dark or
  baking chocolate

Topping

½ cup (125 mL) whipping
  cream
½ cup (125 mL) butter
½ cup (125 mL) white
  sugar

5 tbsp (75 mL) corn syrup
  or golden syrup
½ cup (125 mL) flaked
  almonds

Preheat oven to 400°F (200°C). Combine flour and ground almonds, add sugar and melted butter. Mix well.

Spread mixture in a greased 9 x 13 inch (22 x 33 cm) pan and bake for 10-12 minutes. Cool.

To prepare topping: Place cream, butter, sugar and syrup in heavy-based saucepan. Gently bring to a boil and cook, stirring, for 10 minutes. Add almonds, and still stirring, simmer for 5 minutes.

Increase oven temperature to 375°F (190°C). Spread topping over cooled cookie. Return to oven for 15 minutes. Cool and cut into different shapes.

Melt chocolate in a bowl over a pan of hot water. Dip base of each cookie in chocolate and leave to set.

Makes about 18 (pictured on previous page)

Florentines

6 tbsp (90 mL) butter
½ cup (125 mL) white
  sugar
4 oz (110 g) chopped
  almonds
3 tbsp (45 mL) sultana
  raisins, chopped
5 glacé cherries, chopped
3 tbsp (45 mL) mixed
  candied peel,
  chopped fine
1 tbsp (15 mL) cream
¼ lb (110 g) dark
  chocolate

Preheat oven to 350°F (180°C). Line baking sheets with non-stick baking parchment. Melt butter, add sugar and boil for 1 minute. Stir in remaining ingredients, except chocolate, and mix well.

Drop mixture in small heaps onto baking sheets, keeping them well apart. Bake in oven for 10 minutes, or until golden brown.

Remove from oven and press edges to a neat shape. When they begin to firm, transfer to a rack and cool.

Melt chocolate in a bowl over a pan of hot water. Allow to cool until fairly thick. Spread backs of cookies thickly with chocolate. Using a fork, mark chocolate with wavy lines and leave to set.

Makes about 14

Chocolate Rum Layer Cake

1¼ cups (310 mL)
  all-purpose flour
5 tbsp (75 mL) cocoa
  powder
½ tsp (2 mL) salt
2 tsp (10 mL) baking
  powder
¾ cup (185 mL) firmly
  packed brown sugar
2 eggs, separated

½ cup (125 mL)
  vegetable oil
½ cup (125 mL) milk
½ tsp (2 mL) vanilla
  extract
¼ cup (60 mL) rum
1¼ cups (310 mL)
  whipping cream
3-4 oz (90-110 g)
  chocolate, grated

Preheat oven to 350°F (180°C).

Sift together flour, cocoa powder, salt and baking powder and stir in sugar. Mix together egg yolks, oil, milk and vanilla extract and beat with flour mixture to a smooth batter.

Whisk egg whites until stiff and peaking, then fold into batter with metal spoon.

Divide mixture between two 8 inch (20 cm) round greased and lined pans and bake for about 30 minutes until well risen and firm to the touch. Turn out and cool on wire rack.

Return cold cakes to clean pans and sprinkle with rum. Let stand until rum has been absorbed.

Whip cream until thick. Use a little less than half to sandwich the two layers together, then transfer cake to a serving plate. Spread remaining cream over top and sides. Press chocolate onto sides and sprinkle over top.

Serves 8 (pictured on previous page)

Chocolate Orange Layer Cake

ingredients for
  1 Genoese sponge
  (see Cupid's
  Chocolate Cake
  recipe, page 67)
5 tbsp (75 mL) butter

1¼ cups (310 mL) icing
  sugar
few drops orange extract
1 tbsp (15 mL) milk
1 lb (450 g) dark or
  semisweet baking
  chocolate

Prepare Genoese sponge following instructions in Cupid's Chocolate Cake. Bake in greased, lined 8 inch (20 cm) round cake pan for 40 minutes or until done. Turn sponge cake out of pan and allow to cool. Cut it crosswise into 3 equal layers.

Cream butter until soft and beat in icing sugar, a little at a time, until soft and fluffy. Add orange extract and milk, and blend thoroughly.

Measure 1-1½ oz (30-40 g) chocolate and melt it gently until liquid. Beat it into buttercream mixture.

Divide mixture and spread half over bottom layer and half over middle layer of cake. Place upper layer of cake on top.

Place a heatproof bowl in a pan of hot water. Chop remaining chocolate, put in bowl and stir it until melted. Spread chocolate over top and sides of cake. Decorate, if desired, with whipped cream or bought cake decorations.

Serves 6-8

Mandarin Surprise Layer Cake

1½ quantities ingredients
  for Genoese sponge
  (see Cupid's Chocolate
  Cake recipe, page 67)

finely grated rind of
  1 orange

Filling and Topping

½ cup (125 mL) ground
  almonds
⅔ cup (165 mL) icing
  sugar
8 oz (225 g) canned
  mandarins in syrup
few drops green food
  coloring

1¼ cups (310 mL)
  whipping cream
6 oz (180 g) chocolate,
  finely grated to
  form curls

Preheat oven to 375°F (190°C).

Prepare Genoese sponge following instructions in Cupid's Chocolate Cake, replacing the cocoa powder with an equal quantity of flour, and adding orange rind with flour.

Transfer mixture to a greased and lined 10 inch (25 cm) round cake pan and bake in preheated oven for about 1 hour, until firm to the touch. Turn out onto a wire rack to cool.

To prepare filling: Combine almonds and sugar. Drain mandarins, reserving syrup, and add enough syrup to almonds and sugar to form a spreading consistency. Tint with a few drops of green food coloring, if desired.

Whip cream until just thick. Reserve 18 mandarin segments for decoration, chop remainder and add to half of the cream. Split cold sponge into 3 layers. Spread 2 bottom layers with almond mixture and mandarin cream. Re-assemble cake.

Pipe remaining portion of cream over top of cake and decorate with mandarin segments and chocolate curls.

Serves 12

Black Forest Cake

Soak the cherries overnight in kirsch for sumptuous results.

6 eggs, separated
1 cup (250 mL) sugar
¾ cup (185 mL)
  vegetable oil
¾ cup (185 mL) water
1⅔ cups (415 mL) self-
  rising flour
1¼ cups (310 mL) chocolate
  milk powder
1 jar pitted morello
  cherries
1 tbsp (15 mL)
  cornstarch
¾ cup (185 mL) kirsch
2½ cups (625 mL)
  whipping cream
caraque (see recipe
  page 72) for decoration

Cake

Preheat oven to 350°F (180°C).

Beat egg yolks with sugar until light and frothy. Add oil and water, beating constantly.

Sift flour and chocolate milk powder. Add to egg mixture and combine well.

Beat egg whites until soft peaks form. Fold into chocolate mixture. Pour into a greased 9 inch (23 cm) springform cake pan. Bake in 350°F (180°C) oven for 1 hour. Allow to cool in pan.

Filling

Drain cherries, reserving syrup. Pour kirsch over cherries, cover and soak overnight or as long as possible. Drain again, reserving kirsch. Combine reserved syrup and cornstarch in a small saucepan. Add cherries and cook until thickened. Allow to cool.

Assembly

Cut cake in half, brush with reserved kirsch. Reserve 12 cherries and spread the remaining cherry mixture on one cake layer. Place second layer on top and spread both with whipped cream. Cover top and sides with chocolate caraque. Decorate with reserved cherries and dust cake with sifted icing sugar just before serving.

Serves 8-10

Mint Chocolate Layer Cake

ingredients for
1 Genoese sponge
  (see Cupid's Chocolate
  Cake recipe)
2 cups (500 mL)
  whipping cream
2-3 tbsp (30-45 mL)
  Crème de Menthe
  (optional)
4 oz (110 g) milk
  chocolate
mint chocolate thins
  to decorate

Preheat oven to 375°F (190°C).

Prepare Genoese sponge cake following instructions in Cupid's Chocolate Cake recipe. Transfer mixture to two greased and lined 8 inch (20 cm) shallow round cake pans and bake in preheated oven for 25-30 minutes. Cool on a wire rack.

Whip cream until it is just thick and fold in Crème de Menthe, if using. Reserve a little cream for decoration and use rest to sandwich cake layers and to frost sides.

Melt chocolate in a bowl over a pan of hot, but not boiling, water and spread over top of cake. Pipe a border of rosettes around the top of cake with reserved cream.

Press mint chocolate thins onto side of cake, and decorate top between rosettes with mint chocolate thins cut in half diagonally.

Note: Mint Chocolate Layer Cake can also be decorated with coffee-flavored truffles. Melt 2 oz (60 g) plain chocolate in a bowl over hot, but not boiling, water and stir in a little coffee extract to flavor and thicken chocolate. Then add enough ground almonds to form a stiff paste. Shape mixture into small balls and toss in chocolate vermicelli or cocoa powder.

Serves 8

Chocolate Mint Layer Cake

Cream filled cakes can be messy to cut. This recipe explains how to make life much easier – by cutting the top two layers in advance.

4 oz (110 g) puffed rice cereal
4 oz (110 g) dark or
  semisweet baking
  chocolate
1 tbsp (15 mL) butter
1¼ cups (310 mL)
  whipped cream
peppermint extract
green food coloring
mint leaves or geranium
  leaves to decorate

Melt chocolate in a bowl over hot, not boiling, water. Place puffed rice in a bowl. Pour on melted chocolate and mix well with metal spoon.

Use butter to grease bases of three 7 inch (18 cm) flan rings (or pie plates). Press puffed rice and chocolate into base of flan rings, making a layer about ¼ inch (0.5 cm) thick.

Using a sharp knife, cut two of the chocolate layers into 6 wedges each. Leave remaining layer whole. Place each flan tin in a plastic bag, seal and refrigerate for 5 hours, or overnight.

Remove chocolate flan layers from flan rings. Add 3 drops peppermint extract and 2 drops green food coloring to whipped cream. Mix well so that cream is an even, pale green color.

Spread half of cream over whole flan layer. Arrange layer of 6 wedges on top. Spread remaining cream on top. Place remaining 6 wedges on top lined up with wedges on layer below. Leave small gap between slices so that cream shows between them.

Decorate cake with fresh mint or geranium leaves.

Serves 6

Chocolatine Layer Cake

This cake is based on a Genoese sponge cake foundation. The decoration is elaborate but it makes the cake a good party piece.

1½ quantities of ingredients for Genoese sponge (see recipe Cupid's Chocolate Cake)
2 tbsp (30 mL) cocoa powder
1 lb (450 g) dark or semisweet baking chocolate
¾ cup (185 mL) butter
2½ cups (625 mL) icing sugar
¼ cup (60 mL) Grand Marnier
5 tbsp (75 mL) apricot jam
½ cup (125 mL) whipping cream, whipped

Preheat oven to 375°F (190°C). Prepare Genoese mixture following the recipe instructions. Pour mixture into greased and lined 10 inch (25 cm) cake pan and bake for 45 minutes or until cooked. Cool on a wire rack.

Prepare piece of waxed paper for chocolate shapes by drawing a circle 2½ inches (6.5 cm) in diameter, and 16 triangles 3½ inches (8.5 cm) long and 1½ inches (4 cm) wide at the widest part.

Grate 4 oz (110 g) chocolate and set aside. Break remaining chocolate into bowl and stand it over pan of hot, but not boiling, water until melted. Make sure that bottom of bowl does not touch hot water, as this can cause chocolate to thicken. Do not stir chocolate.

Cream butter until light and fluffy. Add icing sugar gradually, beating well, then beat in Grand Marnier. Add a little of the melted chocolate to flavor and color it lightly.

Make a waxed paper cone, fill it with a little melted chocolate and snip the pointed end. Pipe chocolate onto the drawn outlines and fill shapes with chocolate 'squiggles', refilling the bag with melted chocolate when necessary. Leave until set.

Split cold cake into 2 layers and sandwich with apricot jam and whipped cream.

Reserve ⅓ of prepared buttercream for piping and spread rest over top and sides of cake. Press grated chocolate onto sides.

Place reserved buttercream into a piping bag fitted with a star nozzle and pipe 16 large rosettes around top of cake. Remove the set chocolate triangles from the paper with a palette knife and arrange them on the cake in a cartwheel fashion, slanting each one on a piped rosette.

Pipe a circle of buttercream around tip of chocolate triangles and lay chocolate circle on top.

Serves 16

Cupid's Chocolate Cake

Genoese Sponge Cake

4 eggs
½ cup (125 mL) granulated sugar
5 tbsp (75 mL) unsalted or clarified butter
⅔ cup (165 mL) flour
1 tbsp (15 mL) cocoa powder

Topping

1¼ cups (310 mL) whipping cream
few drops vanilla extract
8 oz (225 g) milk chocolate

Preheat oven to 375°F (190°C). To make Genoese sponge, place eggs and sugar in a bowl over a pot of hot water. Whisk until mixture leaves a trail when you hold up whisk. Remove from heat and continue whisking until cool.

Melt butter and leave until cool but not set. Sift flour and cocoa together. Gently fold small quantities alternately of flour and melted butter into egg mixture, finishing with flour.

Pour mixture into 2 lined, greased, heart-shaped cake pans. Bake for 25-30 minutes until cooked. Test by lightly touching center of cakes. When cakes feels firm and there are no finger marks, they are cooked. Also, cakes should have shrunk away slightly from sides of pans. Cool cakes on wire rack.

Whip cream with vanilla. Reserve some whipped cream for decoration and use rest to sandwich the cold cakes.

Make chocolate curls for decoration by scraping milk chocolate bar with vegetable peeler. Melt remaining chocolate in a bowl over pan of hot, but not boiling, water and spread over top and sides of cake.

When chocolate has set, pipe cream in a heart shape on top of cake. Pipe three lines of cream from top to bottom of cream heart and top with chocolate curls. Decorate with a red ribbon if desired.

Note: For extra zing, sprinkle 3 tbsp (45 mL) rum or Tia Maria over cooked cakes before decorating.

Serves 6-8

HANDMADE
CHOCOLATES

Chocolate-making equipment

Double boiler
A two-tiered system of melting chocolate, fillings or delicate sauces without direct contact with heat. A heat-proof bowl or saucepan is placed above a saucepan half-filled with hot water. Make sure water does not come up as high as bottom of bowl or saucepan containing chocolate.

Bain-marie
A metal vessel half-filled with hot water, in which bowls of chocolate or fillings are gently cooked or melted.

Electric frying pan
Useful as a version of the bain-marie, particularly if you want to melt several different types of chocolate or fillings at once. Half-fill frying pan with hot water and stand small heatproof bowls in water.

Small heatproof bowls
For use in melting chocolate in electric frying pan.

Thermometer
Certain recipes, such as fondant, praline and fudge, require careful temperature control. Use a candy thermometer as it measures the higher temperatures required in chocolate making.

Dipping sticks and spoons
Used for dipping pieces of fruit or nuts into melted chocolate to be coated all over.

Oils and extracts
Chocolates can generally only be flavored with oil-based flavorings and extracts, because the addition of any water to melted chocolate spoils the appearance, taste and consistency of the finished product.

Colorings
Again, only oil-based colors should be used to tint chocolate. Fine paint brushes are invaluable for delicate coloring effects.

Molds
A wide range of molds are now available so you can make your chocolates shell-shaped, heart-shaped, bell-shaped or flower-shaped – or take your pick from more conventional chocolate molds. See Chocolate Molding recipe for the best results.

Chocolate Tempering

As this book is devoted to chocolate, it is important to mention chocolate tempering. During tempering, it is essential that not one drop of water should come into contact with the chocolate.

In all the recipes in this section, compound or couverture (coating) chocolate has been used, unless otherwise stated.

It is only necessary to temper chocolate when using it for molding or dipping. For any fillings, pure chocolate or baking chocolate can be used without tempering.

Break chocolate into small pieces and place it in a bowl over hot, not boiling, water. Stir occasionally until it is melted and the temperature is 115°F-118°F (46°C-48°C). If this temperature is exceeded, the chocolate is ruined.

Remove the bowl from saucepan and set in ice water, stirring carefully until the chocolate begins to set on the bottom. Then warm the chocolate carefully over hot water (not on stove) until the temperature is: dark chocolate, 88°F (31°C); milk chocolate, 84°F (29°C); white chocolate, 84°F (29°C). If the above temperatures are exceeded, the tempering process should begin again.

Note: in mid-summer months, compound chocolate will set perfectly well but will not have such a glossy appearance.

Filled Chocolates
1 Quarter fill mold with chocolate

Chocolate Molding

Solid chocolates
1 Molds must be clean and dry
2 Fill mold with melted chocolate and tap on table to remove air bubbles
3 Chill mold in freezer until set (about 3 minutes)
4 Tap mold gently to remove chocolates.

Filled chocolates
1 Quarter fill the mold with melted chocolate and tap to remove air bubbles
2 Brush chocolate evenly up the sides of the mold to make a shell and freeze until set (approximately 2 minutes)
3 Add filling such as truffle, nuts, fondant, fruit, etc
4 Fill to top with melted chocolate and tap gently to remove air bubbles
5 Return to freezer to set (about 3 minutes), remove and gently tap out chocolates.

Marbled chocolates
1 Spoon a little white and dark chocolate separately into dish
2 With a teaspoon swirl the white into the dark chocolate to make marble patterns
3 Gently scoop up chocolate and fill mold evenly
4 Tap to remove air bubbles and freeze until set (about 3 minutes). Then tap out chocolates.
Note: 8 oz (225 g) compound chocolate makes 25-30 chocolate shells or 10-20 whole chocolates, depending on the size of the molds.

Caraque

2 oz (60 g) dark chocolate
walnut-size piece of butter

Melt chocolate and butter in top of double boiler. Allow to cool a little, then pour onto hard flat surface, such as marble or tile. Spread it out quickly with a spatula.

When chocolate is firm but not completely hard, scrape the surface with a heavy kitchen knife or a spatula warmed in hot water.

Put the blade at a 45° angle to the table and push. Chocolate with form long cylindrical curls which will break very easily so treat with care. Avoid touching caraque if possible as the warmth of your hands will melt the chocolate very quickly.

2   Brush chocolate up sides, then freeze

3   Add small amount of filling

4   Fill to top with chocolate

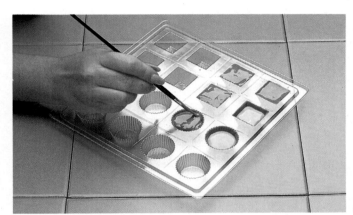

5   Carefully level off chocolate

Marbled Chocolates

Boiled Fondant

Boiled fondant is the ultimate fondant for chocolate making, but it does require a lot of time and care. The simple fondant method (see following recipe) can be used in place of boiled fondant. Boiled fondant is available from certain cake specialty shops.

2¼ cups (560 mL) sugar
5 tbsp (75 mL) water
1 tbsp (15 mL) liquid glucose

1 Sprinkle a large marble slab or large baking sheet with water.
2 Place all ingredients into saucepan over medium heat and stir, continuously brushing down sides of saucepan with wet pastry brush to remove sugar crystals, until sugar dissolves.
3 Bring syrup to a boil over high heat and continue boiling until a drop of syrup in saucer of cold water forms a soft ball (approximately 233°F-240°F or 112°C-116°C).
4 Remove saucepan from heat and quickly dip base into cold water to stop the cooking.
5 Pour syrup onto prepared marble slab or baking sheet and leave to cool for a few moments.
6 With a dampened metal scraper, turn outsides of the mixture towards the middle to allow mixture to cool evenly. Continue this action until mixture has a yellowish tinge.
7 Using a figure-eight motion, work mixture with a wooden spoon or spatula for 5-10 minutes until it becomes opaque, crumbly and white in color.
8 With wet hands, form mixture into a ball and knead for about 10 minutes until it is smooth, white and plastic to the touch. Leave covered in refrigerator overnight for better results.
9 Fondant may be stored indefinitely in an airtight container in the refrigerator.

Alternative method

Prepare fondant as above to end of step 5. When fondant has cooled slightly, beat with a strong electric mixer (i.e. 350-500 watt) until mixture becomes crumbly and white in color. Then continue steps 8 and 9.

Boiled Fondant
1   Brush down sides of pan to remove sugar crystals

2   Test for soft ball stage by dropping mixture into saucer of water

3   Pour syrup onto prepared marble slab

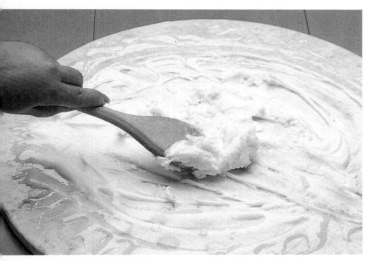

4   *Work mixture with a metal spatula until it thickens*

5   *Using a wooden spoon, work mixture in a figure-eight motion until it becomes opaque*

6   *Form mixture into a ball and knead until it is plastic to the touch*

Simple Fondant

2½-2¾ cups (625-685 mL)
  icing sugar
1 egg white
1 tbsp (15 mL) liquid
  glucose, warmed
extra icing sugar for
  kneading

Place icing sugar, egg white and glucose in a bowl and mix together to form a firm dough. Turn out onto a board well-dredged with the extra icing sugar. Knead until easy to handle.

Place in refrigerator in airtight container for storage.

Add coloring and flavors of your choice and use fondant for fillings and centers for chocolates.

This fondant can be used for molding roses and shapes for chocolate decorations.

Easter Eggs and Chocolate Boxes

Cut mold in two for easy handling. Clean and dry molds thoroughly.

Fill both halves of mold with melted chocolate and freeze until outside edge has hardened (about 3-4 minutes). Pour out liquid chocolate and set aside. Return mold to freezer to set. Excess chocolate can be used for further molding or will keep for a later date.

To join halves, cement edges together with a little melted chocolate, or pipe edges with melted chocolate or icing using piping bag with fluted tube.

Before joining halves together, eggs may be filled with small eggs or chocolates.

This method can be used for making chocolate boxes.

Note: Quantity of chocolate depends on size of molds and number of eggs or boxes required.

Melt chocolate in a small container over hot water

Add peppermint flavoring

Paint the back of each leaf with chocolate

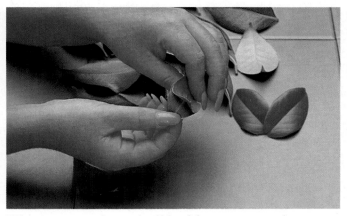

When set, gently peel off leaf from stem end

Chocolate Peppermint Leaves

Chocolate leaves are the perfect finishing touch for cakes or desserts. They also make an elegant decoration for a plate of chocolates for your dinner party. Choose leaves that are perfect, shiny and heavily veined such as rose, orange, camellia or gardenia leaves, or ivy.

5 oz (150 g) dark
   compound chocolate
2-3 drops peppermint
   oil flavoring
leaves of your choice

Clean and dry leaves. Melt chocolate by standard method and add 2-3 drops peppermint oil flavoring. Paint the back of each leaf with chocolate, place on tray and freeze until set. Gently peel off leaves from chocolate starting with stem end.

To vary, use white chocolate colored with oil-based food coloring and flavor with other flavors, for instance pale pink leaves with strawberry oil flavoring.

Put almonds in oven to warm through

Dissolve sugar in water, stirring and brushing down sides of pan

Almond Praline

12 oz (340 g) blanched
   almonds, slivered
   or chopped
⅔ cup (165 mL) water
2¼ cups (560 mL)
   granulated sugar

Place almonds on tray and put into a preheated 350°F (180°C) oven. Switch oven off and leave almonds there for duration of cooking time of the sugar syrup (about 15-20 minutes).

Thoroughly grease a marble slab or two 9 x 13 inch (22 x 33 cm) pans. In a heavy-based saucepan, over medium heat, dissolve water and sugar, stirring constantly and occasionally brushing down sides of saucepan with a wet pastry brush to remove sugar crystals. When sugar is dissolved, bring to a boil for 15-18 minutes over high heat until mixture is a light caramel shade.

Remove saucepan from heat, dip base into cold water immediately, and quickly add warm almonds. Stir gently and pour straight onto greased marble slab or into pans. Allow to cool, break into bite-sized pieces and store in an airtight container.

Praline powder

This is excellent for filling chocolates. Place praline pieces into a powerful food processor (350-500 watt) and use the strongest blade to reduce praline to a fine powder. Store in an airtight container.

Note: Ready-made peanut brittle can be used instead of praline. Break peanut brittle into pieces and use a processor or blender to reduce to powder.

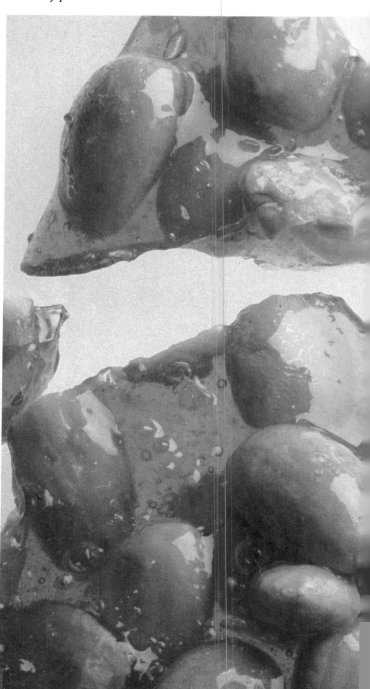

Spread onto a marble slab

When cool, break into bite-sized pieces

Fruit Dipping with Chocolate or Fondant

*1 lb (450 g) berries in
season or glacé fruit
½ quantity boiled fondant
or simple fondant
(see recipe page 74-75)*

*small quantity crystal
sugar for coating or
5 oz (150 g) dark
compound chocolate,
melted*

Wash fruit, pat dry and place on tray.

In a large pan, simmer water over medium heat. Put fondant into a smaller pan and place inside large pan of water. Water should reach as high as the fondant.

Stir fondant continuously until it melts. If it is too thick to form an even coating, add a few drops hot water. Do not heat fondant above 150°F (66°C) or it will become brittle when set.

Holding each piece of fruit by its stalk or by one end, dip it into fondant. Allow excess fondant to drip off, then dip fondant-coated tip of fruit into a bowl of sugar. Place on lined tray and allow to set (approximately 5-10 minutes). Any remaining fondant can be re-used.

Fruit can be dipped in melted chocolate instead of fondant and sugar.

Wash fruit and pat dry

Use dipping forks to dip fruit into melted chocolate

TRUFFLES, CREAMS
AND SOFT CENTERS

Apricot Truffles

14 oz (400 g) white
  compound chocolate
½ cup (125 mL)
  whipping cream
2 oz (60 g) glacé apricots
1 tsp (5 mL) vanilla
  extract
1 tbsp (15 mL) apricot
  extract

Chop 9 oz (250 g) of the chocolate. Put chocolate in bowl over hot water and stir occasionally until melted.

Place cream in saucepan on stove and bring to a boil, stirring constantly. Remove from stove and cool to room temperature. Add cooled cream to melted, cooled chocolate and allow mixture to stand for 20 minutes, then beat with electric mixer until mixture is fluffy and lighter in color. Fold in chopped glacé apricots, vanilla extract and apricot extract.

Refrigerate mixture until firm enough to roll into balls. Shape mixture into small balls and place on foil-lined tray.

Melt remaining chocolate using standard method, as above. Dip truffles in chocolate and allow to set on tray.

previous page: Lemon Coconut Truffles

Chocolate Praline Cinnamon Balls

9 oz (250 g) white
  compound chocolate
½ cup (125 mL)
  whipping cream
4 oz (110 g) praline
  powder (see Almond
  Praline recipe)
1 tsp (5 mL) vanilla
  extract
2 tsp (10 mL) cinnamon
½ cup (125 mL) sugar

Chop chocolate into pieces and put in bowl. Melt over hot water, stirring occasionally until melted. Place cream in saucepan on stove and bring to a boil, stirring constantly. Remove from stove and cool to room temperature.

Add cream to melted chocolate and allow to cool for ½ hour, then beat with electric mixer until mixture is fluffy and lighter in color. Fold in praline powder and vanilla extract. Refrigerate mixture until firm enough to roll into balls.

Mix cinnamon and sugar together. Shape heaped teaspoons of praline mixture into small balls and coat with cinnamon and sugar.

Apricot Truffles

84

Simple Strawberry Creams

4 oz (110 g) cream cheese
1½ cups (375 mL) icing
  sugar
3 drops strawberry
  extract
2 drops pink liquid food
  coloring
½ tsp (2 mL) vanilla
  extract
5 oz (150 g) compound
  chocolate, for molding

Beat together cream cheese and icing sugar until smooth. Add strawberry extract, coloring and vanilla.

Melt chocolate over hot, not boiling, water. Line chocolate molds with chocolate, freeze, and when set fill with strawberry cream.

Seal tops with chocolate and freeze until set.

Note: This is an ideal easy method for soft-centered chocolates. Any flavoring and coloring can be used.

Ten-Minute Truffles

½ cup (125 mL) whipping
  cream
9 oz (250 g) dark
  baking chocolate,
  chopped
3 tbsp (45 mL) Grand
  Marnier or cognac
cocoa powder for dusting
  or crushed nuts
  for rolling

Place cream in saucepan over medium heat and bring to a boil. Take saucepan off stove. Stir in chopped chocolate and allow to melt. Stir gently to combine. Refrigerate until mixture is cool.

Beat at high speed with electric mixer for 2-3 minutes. Add Grand Marnier or cognac. Spoon onto greased tray and freeze until set. Use as a filling for chocolate molds, or roll into balls and dust with cocoa powder, or roll in crushed nuts.

Port and Pistachio Nut Truffles

5 oz (150 g) dark
  compound chocolate
¼ cup (60 mL) unsalted
  butter
½ cup (125 mL) sifted
  icing sugar
1 egg yolk
¼ cup (60 mL) port
2 oz (60 g) chopped
  unsalted pistachio nuts
5 oz (150 g) melted
  chocolate or additional
  pistachio nuts, crushed

Melt chocolate over hot, not boiling, water. Cream together butter and sugar. Allow chocolate to cool and add to mixture, stirring vigorously. Add egg yolk and port and beat until thick and creamy. Stir in nuts, spoon onto waxed paper and refrigerate until firm.

Use as a filling for chocolate molds, or roll into balls and dip in melted chocolate or crushed pistachio nuts.

Lemon Coconut Truffles

½ cup (125 mL) whipping
  cream
9 oz (250 g) white
  compound chocolate,
  chopped
1 tbsp (15 mL) freshly
  grated lemon rind
1½ cups (375 mL)
  shredded coconut
8 drops liquid yellow
  food coloring
1 tbsp (15 mL) milk

Bring cream slowly to a boil, stirring continuously. Remove pan from heat and add chopped chocolate. Let stand until cool (½ hour) and then beat with electric mixer until light and smooth. Blend in lemon rind and ½ cup (125 mL) coconut.

Place teaspoonfuls of mixture on foil-lined tray and freeze until hard. Add yellow coloring to milk. Put remaining coconut in plastic bag, add colored milk and shake vigorously. Roll truffle mixture into balls or pipe into shapes and roll in colored coconut. Keep refrigerated. (Pictured on page 82-83)

Molded Chocolates

Hazelnut Truffles

1 Bring cream to a boil, stirring constantly

2 Add cooled cream to chocolate

3 Add praline mixture

4 Roll mixture into balls and wrap around hazelnuts

5 Dip in melted chocolate

9 oz (250 g) dark compound chocolate
½ cup (125 mL) whipping cream
1 tsp (5 mL) vanilla extract
2 oz (60 g) praline powder (see Almond Praline recipe) or 2 oz (60 g) chopped unsalted, roasted hazelnuts

20-24 whole, roasted hazelnuts
7 oz (200 g) dark compound chocolate for dipping

Chop chocolate and put in bowl over hot water, stirring occasionally until melted. Place cream in saucepan on stove and bring to a boil, stirring constantly.

Remove cream from stove and cool to room temperature. Add cream and vanilla extract to melted, cooled chocolate and allow mixture to stand for about ½ hour. Beat with electric mixer until mixture is fluffy and lighter in color.

Fold in praline powder (or chopped hazelnuts) and refrigerate for ½ hour. Roll mixture into balls around each hazelnut and place on foil-lined tray.

Melt additional chocolate by standard method, coat truffles and allow to set on tray. Alternatively, sandwich truffles between molded shells, or use truffle to fill chocolate molds.

Chestnut Creams

¼ cup (60 mL) unsalted
  butter
2 oz (60 g) compound
  chocolate or baking
  chocolate, chopped
2 oz (60 g) copha,
  chopped

4 oz (110 g) sweetened
  chestnut spread
2 tsp (10 mL) rum
4 oz (110 g) milk
  compound chocolate
  (additional)

Bring butter to room temperature. Melt chopped chocolate and chopped copha over hot water, remove from heat and allow to cool but not set.

Meanwhile, cream butter and beat in chestnut spread and rum. Stir in cooled chocolate mixture.

Melt additional chocolate over hot water. Place 36 colored foil cases on tray and pour ½ tsp (2 mL) melted chocolate into each case, just enough to cover base. Reserve remaining melted chocolate.

Place chestnut mixture into piping bag fitted with fluted tube and pipe swirls of mixture into foil cases.

Trickle reserved melted chocolate over chestnut mixture in cases. Keep refrigerated until serving. (Pictured on page 91)

Passionfruit Creams

½ x 14 oz (400 g or 300 mL)
  can condensed milk
2 passionfruit
3½ cups (875 mL)
  icing sugar
5 oz (150 g) dark or
  white compound
  chocolate

Combine condensed milk, passionfruit pulp and 3 cups (750 mL) icing sugar and mix well to form a firm dough. On a board, thoroughly knead mixture into remaining icing sugar. If mixture is not firm enough to roll into balls, add more icing sugar.

Roll into small balls (big enough to fit into chocolate cases) and refrigerate for ½ hour.

Melt chocolate and use to coat foil cases or molds. Refrigerate until set. If using foil cases, remove them from chocolate when set. Place passionfruit balls into chocolate cases or molds and refrigerate.

Passionfruit Creams

FUDGES, FRUIT, NUTS
AND LIQUEURS

Chocolate Peppermint Shells

2 egg yolks
1/4 cup (60 mL) unsalted
  butter
6 oz (180 g) dark
  compound chocolate,
  chopped
3 drops peppermint oil
  flavoring
5 oz (150 g) dark
  compound chocolate
  (additional)

Place egg yolks into bowl and lightly beat. Cut butter into small pieces.

Place chopped dark compound chocolate in bowl over saucepan of boiling water, and stir until completely melted. Remove bowl from boiling water and gradually blend in butter, stirring well after each addition.

Blend a little of the chocolate mixture with beaten egg yolks and then stir eggs into the chocolate mixture. Stir mixture gently over hot water on very low heat for 3-4 minutes. Add peppermint oil.

Place mixture in freezer for 5 minutes. Remove and allow to set at room temperature.

Molding

Brush shell molds with melted additional chocolate and refrigerate until set.

Fill each shell with chocolate peppermint mixture, allowing enough space to top with melted chocolate. Reserve remaining mixture. Cover top of molds with melted chocolate and refrigerate until set. Remove chocolates from molds.

Cement two shells together with remaining chocolate mixture and decorate.

Hazelnut Coffee Clusters

Crunchy Chocolate Squares

8 oz (225 g) milk or dark
  compound chocolate
4 oz (110 g) praline
  powder (see Almond
  Praline recipe page 78)

Melt chocolate over hot water. Fold in praline powder. Place in square molds and refrigerate until set. Turn out of molds and store.

Note: With the addition of praline powder the chocolate mixture will need to be spooned into molds as quickly as possible as it will be thicker and will set more quickly. Bang mold on counter to spread evenly.

Dale's Delight

1¼ cups (310 mL) light
  corn syrup
1¼ cups (310 mL) sugar
14 oz (400 g or 300 mL)
  can sweetened
  condensed milk

1¾ cups (440 mL)
  whipping cream
4 oz (110 g) unsweetened
  compound chocolate,
  chopped

Line an 8 inch (20 cm) square pan with foil, then grease. Combine all ingredients except chocolate in heavy-based saucepan and place over medium heat, stirring constantly with a wooden spoon until all sugar crystals are dissolved.

Continue cooking for about 45 minutes over low heat, stirring frequently. Add chopped chocolate and cook for another 10-15 minutes, brushing down exposed sides of saucepan with a wet pastry brush while still stirring frequently.

Remove from heat and pour into prepared pan. Allow to firm overnight in refrigerator. Cut into shapes.

Hazelnut Coffee Clusters

5 oz (150 g) chocolate
coffee oil flavoring, to taste
4 oz (110 g) hazelnuts

Melt chocolate over hot, not boiling, water. Add coffee extract. Cement three hazelnuts together at a time with melted chocolate. Allow to set, then dip in melted chocolate. Decorate with hazelnut on top.

Chestnut Creams (recipe page 87) and
Crunchy Chocolate Squares

White Chocolate Nut Fudge

2 cups (500 mL)
   granulated sugar
1¼ cups (310 mL)
   sour cream
4 oz (110 g) white
   compound chocolate,
   chopped
½ tsp (2 mL) salt
3 tbsp (45 mL) liquid
   glucose or light
   corn syrup

1 tsp (5 mL) vanilla
   extract
2 tsp (10 mL) unsalted
   butter
2 oz (60 g) unsalted
   macadamia nuts,
   chopped

In large, heavy-based saucepan, combine sugar, sour cream, chopped chocolate, salt and liquid glucose or syrup. Stir over low heat until chocolate is melted and sugar is dissolved. Bring mixture to a boil, reduce heat and simmer, covered, for 3 minutes.

Remove lid from saucepan and stir frequently until mixture reaches 245°F (118°C), or soft ball stage (about ½ hour). Remove from heat and stir in vanilla and butter. Allow to cool without stirring until lukewarm, then beat vigorously with wooden spoon until fudge is no longer glossy.

Stir in chopped macadamia nuts and press mixture into square or rectangular pan lined with aluminum foil, or use nut-shaped molds. Refrigerate until firm. Unmold or cut into squares.

Note: Other unsalted nuts such as peanuts, hazelnuts or walnuts can be substituted for macadamia nuts.

Chocolate Candy Peel with Cointreau

2 oranges
1⅓ cups (335 mL) sugar
1¼ cups (310 mL) water
½ cup (125 mL) Cointreau

Cut orange into quarters. Peel off skin and discard flesh. Remove all pith from peel with a very sharp knife. Cut skin into long strips and rinse under cold running water.

Bring sugar, water and Cointreau to a boil. Add orange strips and simmer for at least 2 hours. Add a little hot water if syrup becomes frothy. Lift out strips onto cooking rack and flatten with spatula. Leave to crystallize for 3 hours or preferably overnight. Dip strips in melted chocolate. Store in airtight jar until ready for use.

White Chocolate Nut Fudge
1   *Combine sugar, sour cream, chopped chocolate, salt and liquid glucose*

4   *Stir in vanilla and butter*

7   *Press mixture into lined pan*

2 Stir over low heat until dissolved

3 Bring to a boil and simmer until mixture reaches soft ball stage

5 When lukewarm, beat vigorously with wooden spoon until fudge loses its gloss

6 Add chopped nuts

8 When set, cut into squares

White Chocolate Nut Fudge used to fill white chocolate shell in nut-shaped mold

Quick and Easy Chocolate Ginger

½ quantity boiled fondant
  or simple fondant (see
  recipes page 74-75)
5 oz (150 g) dark
  chocolate, melted
20 pieces crystallized
  ginger

Wrap fondant around each piece of ginger. Freeze for 10 minutes until firm. Dip in melted chocolate.

Quick and Easy Chocolate Ginger

Chocolate Hazelnut Fudge

4 oz (110 g) compound
  chocolate
¼ lb (110 g) unsalted
  butter or margarine
14 oz (400 g or 300 mL)
  can sweetened
  condensed milk
3 tbsp (45 mL) corn syrup
  or golden syrup

2½ oz (75 g) roasted,
  unsalted hazelnuts,
  chopped
5 oz (150 g) dark
  compound chocolate
  (for melting)

Place all ingredients except hazelnuts into saucepan and stir over low heat until melted. Bring to a boil, reduce heat and simmer for 15 minutes, stirring constantly until mixture has thickened.

Add chopped hazelnuts, mix well and pour mixture into greased square or rectangular pan. Refrigerate until firm.

Remove from pan and cut into squares or other shapes, or roll into balls and coat with coconut.

Dip in melted chocolate, place on lined tray and allow to set.

Chocolate Hazelnut Fudge

Chocolate Marzipan Roll

1 quantity marzipan (see
  next page) or 14 oz
  (400 g) rolled marzipan
4 oz (110 g) dark
  compound chocolate

orange oil flavoring
  (optional)

If using homemade marzipan, divide paste into two and roll out into 2 rectangles about 1/12th inch (2-3 mm) in thickness. Melt chocolate, add orange oil and spread thinly over the marzipan shapes, leaving 2 inches (5 cm) around edges. Spread only a thin layer of chocolate over marzipan as it will be difficult to roll if it is too thick.

Rolling must be done as the chocolate is setting. If allowed to set, the chocolate will crack when rolling. Starting from longest side of rectangle, roll firmly towards the other longest side.

Wrap marzipan roll in foil and place in refrigerator for 20 minutes. Trim ends and slice roll with a sawing motion into ¼ inch (0.5 cm) pieces, using a serrated knife.

Note: Rolled marzipan is available at some supermarkets.

Marzipan

1½ cups (375 mL) icing sugar
8 oz (225 g) almond meal (finely ground almonds)
2 egg whites

Sift icing sugar into bowl and mix in ground almonds.

Beat egg whites until they begin to foam and cut them into the sifted icing sugar and almonds a little at a time, adding just enough to combine mixture. Work mixture together with one hand, adding a little more egg white if it feels too dry or a little more icing sugar if too moist. Knead paste lightly until it comes away from sides of bowl.

Cherry Liqueurs

½ lb (225 g) fresh cherries or glacé cherries
¼ bottle kirsch or liqueur of your choice
1 tsp (5 mL) invertase
½ quantity boiled fondant or simple fondant (see recipes page 74-75)
7 oz (200 g) dark compound chocolate

Prick cherries and soak in kirsch or other liqueur for 2 hours or preferably overnight. Cherries do not need to be completely covered. Drain and dry thoroughly on paper towels. Leftover kirsch can be re-used.

Add invertase to fondant and wrap around cherries. Dip in melted chocolate and when set, dip again in melted chocolate to completely seal fondant.

Allow 5 days to liquidize. Serve in paper cases.

Note: Invertase is available from certain supermarkets and cake specialty stores.

Cherry Liqueurs

INDEX